The
Wonder
of Word Study

Lessons and Activities to Create Independent Readers, Writers, and Spellers

Lauren Berman Lucht

HEINEMANN
Portsmouth, NH

Heinemann
361 Hanover Street
Portsmouth, NH 03801–3912
www.heinemann.com

Offices and agents throughout the world

Library of Congress Cataloging-in-Publication Data
Lucht, Lauren Berman.
The wonder of word study : lessons and activities to create independent
readers, writers, and spellers / Lauren Berman Lucht.
    p. cm.
Includes bibliographical references.
ISBN 0-325-00811-6 (alk. paper)
  1. Vocabulary—Study and teaching (Elementary). 2. Language arts
(Elementary)—Activity programs. I. Title.
LB1574.5.L835 2006
372.61—dc22   2005024247

Editor: Lois Bridges
Production: Elizabeth Valway
Cover and interior design: Joni Doherty
Cover photography: Megan Boneno
Composition: Publishers' Design and Production Services, Inc.
Manufacturing: Louise Richardson

Printed in the United States of America on acid-free paper
10   09   08   ML   3   4   5

Contents

Foreword

When I served as a superintendent of schools in Manhattan, I realized that teachers remained in their schools very late the night before any of my visits. They redecorated bulletin boards, laminated new charts, and added words to their word walls. Truth be told, I wish they hadn't spent their precious time trying to please me in these ways. Sure, I glanced at these classroom artifacts, but I was more concerned with whether anyone stopped to read and respond to bulletin board displays, ever internalized the literacy strategies on all those charts, or understood how to use known words to learn new ones. I was not after a "one size fits all" curriculum or pedagogy. As a district we had a belief system about how children learn to read and write, but I had no preconceived notions about how any one reading or writing workshop must look, sound, or run. In fact, I was most delighted when teachers designed fresh, original ways of helping students become literate. Bottom line for me, I was looking for literacy teachers who so deeply understood the "why" that they invented their own unique "how." Lauren Berman Lucht was just such a teacher.

Reading Lauren's *The Wonder of Word Study* reminded me of my supervisory visits to her early childhood classroom, only this visit lasted a long time and was filled with a master teacher's articulate explanation of her practice. Reading her chapters on workshop setup, word study inquiries, word study assessment, and the use of poetry and games, written in such a clear and conversational tone, made me realize what I had been missing. Oh, that those supervisory visits could have allowed for such rich debriefing sessions and such professional dialogue.

I was particularly pleased that Lauren included transcripts of important teaching moments. Readers will feel like they are pulling up a chair in her classroom as they read her exact words and the way she responds to the youngsters in her care. I was also thrilled that Lauren composed original poems to support her word study teaching. What a powerful literacy model she is for her students. And as a true professional, Lauren credits her roots in this book, citing the authors and books that have helped spark her thinking. Then too, I delighted in all the visual supports studded throughout her book. All the classroom photographs, meaningful charts, student work samples, assessment tools, game sheets, and scheduling and planning artifacts help turn *The Wonder of Word Study* into a very practical guidebook for primary school educators.

My thanks to Lauren for being such a confident and caring colleague, for taking such good care of her New York City students, and for taking the time to share the joys of her teaching. Just as Lauren graciously opened her classroom door to visitors from near and far, this book will open doors to early childhood teachers interested in wisely introducing word study to their young children.

Shelley Harwayne

Acknowledgments

I'd like to thank all the fabulous teachers that I have had the honor of working with over the past ten years. To my colleagues and friends who have supported me, encouraged me, and advised me during the writing of this book, I want to express my deepest appreciation. To my editor, Lois Bridges, thank you for your constant clarifications and unrelenting patience with me as I took on this challenge. Also, I'd like to especially thank Andrea Lowenkopf and Shelley Harwayne for their enthusiasm and belief in me.

I'd like to thank my parents for recognizing my love for teaching and talent for working with young children, at a very early age.

To my husband, who once told me that I am the only teacher who ever truly inspired him, thank you—for your respect, support, and love for what I do.

Most of all, thank you to all the amazing children I have worked with, who pushed me to challenge you and who believed that learning was the most powerful tool you could posses.

Introduction

Why Teach Word Study?

When children learn to read, a whole new world opens up for them. They can explore new regions, find out information, enter imaginative lands, and much much more. Although it often appears that a child is reading, sometimes they are only decoding the text—using their knowledge of letters and sounds to put a word together. I remember numerous workshops and conferences with parents where that one mom or dad stands up and says, "My five-year-old is reading *The Magic School Bus* series," or "My seven-year-old is reading *War and Peace*." What these parents don't understand is that their child may be able to read the words, but this is not yet *reading*. It reminds me of studying for chemistry in high school when I would read an entire chapter in my textbook and then not remember one thing I learned (or *didn't* learn). Or how about trying to read a passage in a foreign language you are learning? You know how the letters and sounds work together, but you have absolutely no idea what it is that you are reading.

Children need to derive meaning from the words they are reading. They need to learn from and understand the words on the page. Only then can they enjoy the wonder of reading. Through word study, children learn not only to decode text but also to make connections, look for patterns, and discover information among words that will help them to make meaning from what they read.

Even though word study is only one piece of literacy instruction, it is a crucial one. Children will use the information they glean from words automatically, fluently, and with confidence. They will use what they've learned to decode and construct words independently. Teaching a child to become an independent learner is the most powerful tool a teacher can give. When we equip children with the correct tools or strategies for problem solving, they can challenge themselves to read and understand the texts they choose; they can begin to pursue their own interests.

As you take on word study instruction, I suggest some guiding principles for an exciting and successful year:

1. **Assess:** Teaching should be driven by assessment. (This will be discussed further in Chapter 5.)
2. **Familiarize:** Teach from the known to the unknown. Children should begin their learning feeling confident and successful.
3. **Prioritize:** Choose lessons or examples of skills that promote the greatest learning among the student population.
4. **Connect:** Provide many opportunities for children to make links and see connections between sounds, letter clusters, known words, and spelling patterns. A teacher can be a guide to pointing out these connections throughout the day—wherever and whenever they may appear.
5. **Explain:** Teaching points should be brought back to the familiar context of reading and writing. Always point out *why* the lesson is being taught and *how* it can help the students in their reading and writing.
6. **Focus:** Do not allow word study to become too prominent in the classroom—it should be a quick but *focused* part of the daily literature block.
7. **Guide:** Guide the children in being responsible for and invested in their own learning. Allow time for them to ask questions and lead the inquiry.

Word study skills teach students to be more independent spellers, readers, and writers. When these skills are learned children can feel comfortable understanding:

- all sounds of the alphabet including those letters that sometimes make two different sounds (for example: *c*, *x*, and all vowels);
- letter combinations for blends and digraphs such as sh- and dr-;
- letter combinations for word endings such as -ed, -ing, or -ies;
- how the spelling of words can change when you make it plural or past tense; and
- which words can be read from memory (high-frequency words), which words can be read phonetically, and which words can be recognized by finding familiar spelling patterns and chunks.

When children interpret word study as an exploration and investigation of words they see every day, the lesson then becomes an engaging experience.

Integrating Word Study into Your Literacy Curriculum

O ver the years, one of my biggest struggles was finding time to teach everything. Next was finding the *right* time to teach everything. Every year I seem to change my schedule and daily routine—observing the children and taking notes on what was working and, more important, what was *not* working. Sometimes I'd have the class on the rug for too long—watching their faces turn into blank stares as they began to chew on their shoelaces. Other times I'd have them on and off the rug so often the class became chaotic and disorganized, and the children often didn't get to finish their assignments on time. (Doesn't this sound familiar?)

Being a Reflective Teacher

Like all areas of study, word study can be both integrated throughout the curriculum and taught as a separate unit. Just as you would teach reading and writing all day long but find a block of time for specific lessons in both, so would you teach word study. But when I began to include word study as a separate subject area I had a hard time finding its place among the other components of my literacy block.

In following with model workshop structures, I strove to teach a minilesson (a quick lesson to teach something specific) and then have the children practice what I just taught. I had to reflect on my schedule and revise my thinking so that our day made sense to the children and allowed for the most learning.

Many of my word study inquiries come from our shared reading, but trying to fit word study in between shared reading and independent reading interrupted the flow of my reading minilessons. Later I realized I could have two different purposes for my shared reading lessons: first, to model a reading strategy for independent reading; and second, to introduce a new word study inquiry. So, I have found that the best time to incorporate my word study minilessons is right after reading workshop and just before interactive writing. In this way the children can go from the known goal (we learn about words in order to make meaning from our reading) to learning something new. Then we put our learning into practice during interactive writing. Also, it's important to have the children go from a whole-group setting to independent or small-group work. This morning plan allows for the children to be on and off the "meeting area" in a meaningful and practical structure. This is where my learning has come to as of today. It is working in my classroom and I am seeing happy, attentive faces. (And the shoelace nibbling has come to an end.)

To me, good teaching has meant *Reflect and Revise* (R and R): I want to recognize when something is not working and revise it (again and again). Use this idea when integrating word study into your curriculum and find out what works best for you. (See Figures 1–1 and 1–2 for sample schedules.)

Beginning the Lesson

To begin a word study minilesson, I always address the purpose for the lesson. I start by explaining why I have picked the area of study and ask the children if they want to share anything they already know about it. Often an inquiry will come about on its own—something of interest or confusion to the children will arise during a shared reading, read-aloud, or writer's workshop. When that happens, I may tell the class to remember their questions for exploration during the next word study lesson. Or, depending on the class, I may stop and address the inquiry immediately.

After introducing our study for the day, I begin to model what I want the children to be able to do. Say, for example, that I want the children to recognize the -ay sound in the high-frequency word *day*. I may write the word *day* on the board or spell it with magnetic letters. I would ask the class if anyone could think of other words that sound like *day*. As they call them out I could either list the words underneath *day* or spell them with magnetic letters. It's a good idea to use different color markers when listing the words—either writing the initial consonants in one color and the spelling pattern (-ay) in another or simply highlighting the spelling pattern with a bright color. The children always get excited about thinking up new words that sound like the word we are focusing on. Once they are comfortable with recognizing words that rhyme, they are easily able to think of a few on their own. The lesson then becomes a positive and engaging experience for the class. For follow-up lessons, the children may want to come up and spell the words with magnetic letters themselves. Or, I sometimes use the overhead projector and ask the children

Sample Daily Schedule for a K/1 Class

TIME	SUBJECT	FOCUS
8:30–8:45	Morning Meeting	Welcome/Schedule for the day.
8:45–9:00	Shared Reading	Looking at first letter clues to get our mouths ready to say the word.
9:00–9:30	Reading Workshop and Guided Reading	Practice getting our mouths ready when we are stuck on a word.
9:30–9:45	Word Study	Looking at the -ay spelling pattern in words that sound like *day*. List the words.
9:45–10:10	Word Study Workshop (and Guided Word Study)	Practicing making -ay words with different mediums (playdough, glue, water painting, etc.).
10:10–10:30	Interactive Writing	Write the sentence, "Today is Brian's birthday." Highlight the word *day* in both words.
10:30–10:45	Read-Aloud	*Peter's Chair*, by Ezra Jack Keats. What was the lesson that Peter learned at the end of the story?
10:45–11:30	LUNCH and YARD	Respectful play
11:30–12:30	Music	(Teacher's preparation period.)
12:30–1:00	Quiet Time (Keeping the lights off and playing calming music sets a good tone in the room.)	Explore other Ezra Jack Keats books with a partner OR any other picture books.
1:00–1:45	Writing Workshop	All About Books: writing all about members in our community.
1:45–2:15	Math	Making combinations of twenty-five cents—Play "Race for a Quarter."
2:15–3:00	Choice Time	Cooperative Play

All Science and Social Studies curriculum is incorporated throughout the day in either read-alouds, writing workshop, or choice time activities.

FIGURE 1–1: Sample Daily Schedule for a K/1 Class

Sample Daily Schedule for a 2/3 Class

TIME	SUBJECT	FOCUS
8:30–8:45	Morning Meeting	Welcome/Go over homework from yesterday.
8:45–9:00	Shared Writing	Practicing the use of apostrophes while writing a story.
9:00–9:45	Read-Aloud and Independent Reading (and Guided Reading)	What pictures came to your mind while listening/reading the book?
9:45–10:00	Shared Reading	What language in the text gave you the images that you saw in your head? Was it your prior knowledge or specific words?
10:00–10:30	Word Study Workshop (and Guided Word Study)	Looking at how apostrophes are used to show possessives.
10:30–11:30	Writing Workshop	Looking at repetitive language in memoirs and trying it on our own.
11:30–12:30	LUNCH and YARD	Respectful play.
12:30–1:30	Math	Using number strings to add three-digit numbers efficiently.
1:30–2:15	Music/Band	(Teacher's preparation period.)
2:15–3:00	Social Studies	Analyze artifact that was "found" and come up with its possible uses.

FIGURE 1–2: Sample Daily Schedule for a 2/3 Class

to move the letters around while the class watches the large screen. *Alternating your methods while keeping your teaching goals consistent is a good way to motivate the students and heighten their interest.*

The Workshop

The minilesson should be short and specific. The teacher's role is to teach *one* new thing each day. After a ten- to fifteen-minute minilesson, the children are sent off to practice what they have just learned. They can be working in small groups or

FIGURE 1–3: Using Magnetic Letters to Spell a New Word

Words that sound like rain

Maine	mane
train	Jane
grain	lane
Spain	insane
brain	cane
remain	plane
chain	pane
drain	crane
plain	
stain	
faint	
paint	
pain	

FIGURE 1–4: Categorizing Words That Have Two Common Spellings

independently—creating lists, sorting words, and making new words using the newly learned spelling pattern. The teacher can assign or recommend appropriate activities that match the needs of the students so that all children are learning. (See Chapter 8: "Games and Activities for Word Study.") While most children are practicing the inquiry for the day, some may either be reviewing past inquiries or working on more challenging studies of their own. Word study workshop *is* just as it is called: a *workshop*. The children are active, engaged, and reflective. They are playing games, learning how to work cooperatively, and involved in a variety of multisensory activities. The workshop is an opportunity for the teacher to meet the individual students' learning styles. (For example, some students may react best to a computer screen whereas others may prefer blocks with letters made from sand.)

The teacher's role during word study workshop is a crucial one. You can alternate between working with a small, guided, word study group and rotating around the room observing the children and taking notes of their progress. By the end of the workshop, you will be able to assess the success of your mini-lesson and can properly plan for the following day's inquiry.

A Sample of a Beginning Word Study Lesson

TEACHER'S FOCUS: *Reviewing the high-frequency word* stop *from the class' shared reading book and using it to help spell other words.*

Teacher: Let's reread the book *Stop*, by Joy Cowley. (*The whole class reads through the book as the teacher follows their reading with a pointer.*)

Teacher: Great job. Yesterday we began to talk about the word *stop* and how it can help us spell many other words.

Mason: Yeah, like *mop, top* . . .

Teacher: Yes, that's right Mason. But first I'd like someone to come up here and frame the word *stop*. Joe?

Joe: (*puts a moldable piece of wax called a "wikki stick" around the word on one page in the book*)

Teacher: Great, you found it right away. What if he couldn't find it that quickly? What could he have done?

Arianna: He could have read the page again and stopped when he got to the word *stop*. (*Children giggle.*)

Teacher: Yeah, that sounded funny but you're absolutely right. A lot of times we need to go back and reread the page. Hmm . . . but look at where the word is on the pages.

Arianna: Oh, it's the first word.

Teacher: I guess that wouldn't help here. What else could he have done?

Elie: He could look for an *S* 'cause *stop* starts with an *S*.

Teacher: Sure, that would work. Okay, let's move on. We need one more person to come frame *stop* for us. Mariah?

Mariah: (*puts a "wikki stick" around the word* stop *on a new page*)

Teacher: Good job. Let's all first name the letters and then we'll snap them out. Remember to look up here for the word.

Class: S-T-O-P.

Teacher: Now snap it.

Class: S-T-O-P . . . stop! (*snap their fingers while calling out the letters*)

Teacher: Remember when we studied patterns and we talked about the "train cars" [units of pattern]? And each train car stayed the same but repeated over and over again? (*Children nod their heads.*)

Teacher: Well, today we're going to look at the word *stop* a bit like a pattern. As we think of other words that sound like *stop* we're going to figure out which part of the word will stay the same. Remember, words that rhyme are words that sound the same at the end. So which part of *stop* is going to stay the same as we spell new words?

Erica: -op.

Teacher: That's right. -op is the pattern or the chunk that will stay the same. I'm going to put *stop* up here with magnetic letters. Now, let's take away the st- and spell a new word. We'll leave -op on the board because that's the part that you're telling me will stay the same. Lauren?

Lauren: *Hop.*

Teacher: Okay, so what letter should I put in front of the chunk to make it *hop*?

Lauren: *H.*

Teacher: Great, it says *hop*. Another word? Isabella?

Isabella: *Pop?*

Teacher: What letter?

Isabella: *P.*

Teacher: Now it says *pop*. Max?

Max: *Clop.*

Teacher: What does that mean?

Max: It means like the noise a horse makes when it's running.

Teacher: Oh, okay. *Clop*. Let's say that slowly. I hear two sounds. *c-l* at the beginning.

Max: Wait, let me see . . . *c-l . . . op*. *C* or a *K* and an *L.*

Teacher: Let's try them both and see if one looks right. (*spells* clop *with magnetic letters, using a* K *first then a* C)

Teacher: Max, which one looks better to you?

Max: That looks good. The one with the *C.*

Teacher: That's right! It *is* spelled with a *C. Another* one? (*responding to all the hands raised*)

Lily: *Chop.*

Teacher: Ooo . . . that's a tricky one. *ch . . . op*. What letters do I put up for that?

Lily: *SH?*

Teacher: *SH* is . . .

Class: *shh . . .* (*making the sound of sh together*)

Teacher: Yeah, *sh* is *shh*. Can you try again? *ch . . .*

Lily: *CH.*

Teacher: Awesome, Lily. It's *ch-*. Now we spelled chop. See how the chunk -*op* stays the same each time? Avery?

Avery: *Lock.*

Teacher: Let's all say *lock* together slowly.

Class:	*L . . . o . . . ck . . .*
Teacher:	Avery, do you hear how *lock* ends with a "kuh" sound? Now listen to these others: *stop, hop, chop.* (*stressing the sound of the* P *at the end*) Does *lock* sound the same at the end?
Avery:	No.
Teacher:	Good. Keep trying. Try and think of one that has op at the end.
Avery:	*Mop.*
Teacher:	Yes! *Mop* sounds the same as *stop.* What does *mop* begin with?
Avery:	*M.*
Teacher:	Are there *more*? (*Many hands go up and the class continues with a few more words.*)
Teacher:	Lily?
Lily:	*Monopoly.*
Teacher:	Let's all say that. *Mon . . . op . . . o . . . ly.* Yes, it has op in it. I'm going to write that down because it's too long to spell with the magnets. Let's do it together. Stretch out the first part.
Class:	*Mon . . .*
Teacher:	Uh! I heard something that you know! Did you hear it? *Mm-on . . .*
Class:	ON!!
Teacher:	Great. *Mon . . . op . . .* We know *that* part!
Class:	OP!
Teacher:	And the last part *o . . . ly . . .* That's the word *monopoly.* Great, Lily.
Lily:	Look it has -*ly* at the end like *fly* but it doesn't sound like *fly.*
Teacher:	That's right. Look at that. Sometimes the *y* can sound like *i* in *fly* or *e* like in *your* name, Lily. You have -*ly* too! Let's do one more. Arianna?
Arianna:	*Fop.*
Teacher:	What does *fop* mean?
Arianna:	I don't know. Nothing.

Teacher: Is it a word that you know?

Arianna: No.

Teacher: Okay, think of another one.

Arianna: *Stop.*

Teacher: Great! We're back to our special word that we started with. Let's put it up and snap it out. Kyle, can you come up and spell *stop*? What two letters will he be looking for? "*Ss . . . tt . . . ?*"

Class: S-T! (*Kyle spells the word with the magnetic letters.*)

Class: S-T-O-P . . . *Stop!* (*snaps it out*)

Teacher: Let's *stop* here. (*Children giggle.*) If you think of more words, write them down on a Post-it or add the letters to the board. We'll continue tomorrow. For now, it's workshop time. Some of you will be working with our new spelling pattern, -op. The rest will be on the computer or other games. Listen as I call your name and tell you what to work on.

2

The Basics
Ideas for Your Word Study Inquiries

As educators we are not strangers to the words *blends*, *digraphs*, *spelling patterns*, *compound words*, and so on. On the other hand, these terms are often defined and used in various ways. In order to avoid any confusion throughout this book, and after making suggestions for your word study inquiries, I define each unit of study in a "friendly" way that works for my students and me. I also give an example of each term. (For further understanding of these terms I would refer you to *Spelling K–8*, by Diane Snowball and Faye Bolton.)

Suggested Word Study Program

The table in Figure 2–1 offers some suggestions for possible mini-lessons within your word study inquiries. Because suggestions for work on the alphabet, syllables, and rhymes will be discussed in a later chapter on beginning readers, the table only includes inquiries from high-frequency words to contractions. All mini-lessons expand on and add to those learned in previous grades.

How Do I Choose?

It would be nice if we could stick to a calendar and neatly fit all the word study inquiries into each week, but I don't believe that's the most effective way for students to learn. Although you can begin in this way—picking an inquiry and planning your minilessons and workshop activities for the week, I try to look at the following components each week:

● STUDENT WRITING—one of the best ways to see what the children need help with is to look at their writing. How are they spelling words? Do they know their sounds? Do they know how to

Suggested Word Study Program Chart

INQUIRY	KINDERGARTEN	FIRST	SECOND	THIRD
High-Frequency Words	and, it, not, me, the, ball, all, like, in, you, are, going, went, see, to, at, play, yes, stop, up, said, can, I, car, not, did, this, am, there, an, be, we, on, and but	because, before, can't, friend, don't, girl, myself, best, boy, today, cold, with, does, every, fine, from, give, great, has, his, hold, if, inside, jump, light, little, big, look, made, nice, want, one, park, play, read, said, school, show, something, soon, start, that, them, thing, your, and work	animal, another, anything, around, became, become, children, everything, everyone, found, having, hear, heart, knew, know, learn, leave, large, money, morning, people, picture, started, seen, short, were, where, water, there, their, together, and without	again, against, almost, already, although, answer, beautiful, between, caught, certain, clothes, couldn't, different, either, enough, half, heard, heavy, instead, important, often, probably, several, should, special, thought, wouldn't, through, throw, trouble, and world
Spelling Patterns	and, at, all, an, ell, ent, id, ill, in, it, ip, to, ug, ice, and ay	ack, ank, ap, ar, ash, aw, eg, en, est, et, ick, ing, ink, ip, ock, on, ump, unk, un, up, ake, ate, ave, and ine	ight, uck, ide, oke, ike, ale, ame, ime, ace, ade, ore, ee, oo, ai, silent e, and long e	atch, itch, etch, otch, oa, ie, ea, and oi
Compound Words	Recognition of a compound word	homework, bathroom, classroom, birthday, upstairs, downstairs, today, bedroom, toothbrush, workshop, backpack, afternoon, into, butterfly, workbook, inside, and outside	because, understood, understand, something, grandmother, grandfather, tonight, rainbow, weekend, newspaper, good-bye, everywhere, everyone, postman, mailman, sometime, airplane, toothpaste, daylight, sunlight, and sunshine	midnight, nighttime, moonlight, basketball, baseball, football, fireplace, fireman, earring, policeman, and suitcase

Word Endings	-s, -ing, and -ed	-y, -er, and -est	-ly, -es, -ful, '-s, and -s'	-y . . . -ies, and -y . . . -ed
Blends	br-, dr-, tr-, gr-, sp-, and st-	bl-, cl-, fl-, gl-, pl-, sl-, cr-, sm-, sn-, sk-, sw-, and str-	pr- and fr-	scr-, spr-, thr-, and squ-
Digraphs	sh-, ch-, and th- in the beginning of words	sh, ch, and th in any spot in a word	wh- and ph-	
Homophones	to/two/too	dear/deer, write/right, won/one, sea/see, son/sun, for/four, I/eye, and know/no	there/their/they're, some/sum, ant/aunt, ate/eight, be/bee, been/bin, hear/here, its/it's, our/hour, whole/hole, high/hi, hair/hare, sent/cent, tail/tale, by/bye/buy, so/sew, week/weak, road/rode, beat/beet, blue/blew, sail/sale, wood/would, mail/male, witch/which, meat/meet, and new/knew	aloud/allowed, close/clothes, great/grate, guessed/guest, pear/pair, passed/past, you're/your, plane/plain, threw/through, stair/stare, where/wear, wait/weight, fair/fare, bear/bare, ball/bawl, weather/whether, and main/mane
Contractions	I'm, Mr, Mrs, and Ms.	Dr., can't, don't, isn't, it's, s, let's, won't, we're, that's, and didn't	I'd, I've, he's, she's, I'll, he'll, she'll, we'll, and isn't	they've, they'll, that'll, you'll, it'll, you're, aren't, haven't, wasn't, doesn't, could've, couldn't, where's, and who's

FIGURE 2–1: Suggested Word Study Program Chart

take words they've learned and use them to spell new words? Are they spelling high-frequency words correctly? Are there specific confusions among the majority of the students? Are there a few students who still don't seem to incorporate the classroom learning into their writing? (This would make for a good *guided word study* group.)

● SHARED READING— a great place to look for word study inquiries. Choose the class poem or a favorite big book and find an inquiry to teach. Does the shared reading have rhyming words? Are there a lot of words that end with -ed? Do many of the words start with sh-? This can go in reverse as well. You can plan to teach an inquiry and then pull out a good shared reading piece with that particular word study inquiry in it. For example: If you recognize that the class knows the word *can* but is spelling words such as *man*, *ant*, or *planet* incorrectly, you can read Joy Cowley's *Dan the Flying Man* (1983 Shortland Publications) and review words that have the -an spelling pattern.

● CHILDREN'S NAMES— if you're lucky enough to have students who have

The alphabet: the letters we use to spell all our words.

Syllables: parts of a word that can be broken up into "claps." For example, *class-room* (2 claps). (For older students I add that each syllable must have at least one vowel in it.)

Rhyming: words that sound the same at the end. For example, *drop/shop*. (It's important to distinguish between words that *start* the same and words that *sound* the same. In the younger grades, many children get confused and consider words such as *blue/black* as rhyming. They hear the bl- in the beginning of both words and recognize the commonality as words that sound the same.)

High-frequency words: words that we see in our reading and writing a lot. ("Quick and easy words.") There are many lists of the fifty to one hundred most frequently used words out there—I recommend using the one that makes the most sense to your student population as a basis.

Spelling patterns: any group of letters that stay together, in the middle or end of words, to help us spell many other words. For example: -en, -ike, or ea. (I consider digraphs and spelling patterns to be two separate inquiries—see my definition for *digraph*.)

Compound words: two words that come together to create a new word— both having some sort of relationship with the other. For example, *bath-room* (the room where you bathe) or *bowtie* (a tie in the shape of a bow). Children have a difficult time understanding why words such as *visitor* are not compound words. Although not always so easily explained, it's good to try to come up with a rule about compound words alongside your students—they will better understand the definition if they help to create it.

Suffixes (or word endings): a spelling pattern that you can add on to the end of a word to change the meaning just a little bit. For example: *funny →funniest* or *swim → swimming*.

Blends: a group of consonant letters that come together in the beginning of a word but let you hear each letter on its own. For example, bl- in *blank* or spr- in *sprinkler*.

Digraphs: a group of consonant letters that come together in the beginning of a word to make only one sound. For example, ch- in *children* or sh- in *shine*.

Homophones: words that sound the same but are spelled differently and mean different things. For example, *sun/son*.

Contractions: the shortcut for a word. Sometimes the shortened word has an apostrophe to hold the place for the missing letters and sometimes it has a period. For example, *can't* or *Mr*.

interesting spellings of their names, you can begin an inquiry by looking at these names. I always get excited when I have students with names such as Max (sound of an *x*), Knox (silent *k* before the *n*), Thaddeus (th- digraph), Travis (tr- blend), Shianne (sh- digraph), Kyle (silent *e* at the end), or Lily (-ly ending). Each time we read or write a word with a th- or an -ly the class remembers: "Th- like Thaddeus!" Or "-ly like at the end of Lily's name!" These inquiries often become the most popular and the most successful.

● ASSESSMENTS—formal or informal. As you record observations and take notes during reading or writing, you may notice small groups or the majority of the class all struggling with the same words. This would be a good time to introduce a new inquiry. You may notice that many children are trying to write words like *dress*, or *drink* and are using a gr- or jr- at the beginning. This would become your study for the week.

● INTEREST—particular themes or science and social studies units are also great places to introduce word study. My class studies frogs every spring. While using the word *frog* in our reading and writing every day, we began to look at the -og spelling pattern. While *frog* went on the word wall as a word we needed a lot, we came up with many other words that we could spell from *frog* (*log*, *jog*, *smog*, *program*, etc.).

A Sample of an Advanced Word Study Lesson

TEACHER'S FOCUS: *To recognize the spelling pattern -ow in words and understand how it can make two different sounds.*

Teacher:	I was noticing that our poem this week has lots and lots of words with -ow in them. Can anyone come up and point to one word with -ow?
Takuma:	*Snow.*
Teacher:	Yes, *snow* has -ow in it. Any others?
Elie:	*Snowball.*
Teacher:	Yes, good, *snowball* has -ow. But *snowball* has the word *snow* in it, which Takuma already gave us. Can anyone find any others that are different than snow?
Lauren:	*Show.*
Teacher:	Great! *Show* has -ow.
Erica:	*Plow.*
Teacher:	Yes, *plow* also has -ow. But isn't it interesting how *plow* sounds different than *snow*? They both end in -ow but sound different?
	(*Children nod.*)
Teacher:	Sometimes -ow can make an *ou* sound like in *plow* and sometimes it can make an *o* sound like in *snow*. Can anyone think of other words that they know that have -ow in them? (*pulls out a chart tablet and markers*)
Kyle:	*No.*
Teacher:	*No* like in "No, I don't want to" or *know* like in "I *know* that one"?
Kyle:	No like in "*No*, I don't want to."
Teacher:	Kyle, how do you spell *no*?
Kyle:	N-O.
Teacher:	Does that word have -ow in it?
Kyle:	Oh! So, the other one?
Teacher:	(*laughs*) Yes, Kyle, the other kind of *know* has -ow. It looks like this.
Jack:	It has a silent *k*.
Teacher:	Yes. Let's make a chart of words that we see in the poem or words that we can think of with -ow.

Jonathan:	*Although*.
Teacher:	Oh, that word does have the *o* sound but it's not spelled with -ow. It looks like this. (*writes it on the wipe-off board to show the students how it looks different*)
Teacher:	Jack?
Jack:	*Blow*.
Teacher:	Great. What two letters?
Jack:	B-L.
Teacher:	*Blow*. Good. Elie?
Elie:	*Wow*.
Teacher:	*Wow*. Good—that one goes over here under the words that have the *ou* sound.
Libby:	Yeah, like sometimes you write *wow* on our home-work.
Teacher:	That's right. Sometimes I do.
Max:	*Bow* like "take a *bow*."
Arianna:	I was thinking of that but I thought it says *bow* (long *o* sound).
Teacher:	That's interesting. Let's write *bow* under *wow* and now I'll write *bow* under *blow*. They look the same.
Erica:	Yeah, but they can be two different things.
Teacher:	They *can* mean two different things. They have a special name. They're called a homograph. That's two words that are spelled the same but sound dif-ferent and mean two different things. Like *wind* (crank up) and *wind* (air gusts).
Kyle:	But how do you know which it is?
Teacher:	I think you would have to listen to the rest of the sentence.
Kyle:	Oh, yeah.
Teacher:	Isabella?
Isabella:	*Dough*.
Teacher:	Like *playdough*?
	(*Isabella nods yes.*)

Teacher:	That one would go up here with *although*. David?
David:	*Growl?*
Teacher:	*Growl!* David, do you know which side that would go on?
David:	Under *ou*.
Teacher:	Yeah, because the -ow makes an *ou* sound like *owl*.
Teacher:	Let's take a look at -ow. Sometimes an -ow makes the *o* sound like these words. Let's read these words together.
Class:	*Know, tow, bow, blow.*
Teacher:	Sometimes an -ow makes the *ou* sound, like in these words:
Class:	*Now, owl, how, wow, plow, bow, growl.*
Teacher:	What we're going to do today is we're going to go on an -ow hunt. You're going to pick a partner and take one of these sheets. On the top of your sheet it says to look for words with -ow in them. Then over here on the side there's two columns or boxes. The first one says, "These words sound like *o*." The other side says, "These words sound like *ou*."
Mason:	We could look on the word wall.
Teacher:	Yes, if there are any words with -ow on there. You and your partner should get a clipboard and walk around the room, hunting for -ow words. Try your best to read the words you find so you can put them in the right boxes. If it sounds like *o* like in *blow* you'll write the word here (*points to the first column*). If it sounds like *ou* like in *wow* you'll write it here (*points to the second column*). If you are done searching for words and you want to just add words you think of on your own, that's great! You can look in books, on our charts and posters, around the room, anywhere you can find words.
Mariah:	We could look in the poem.
Teacher:	Yes, you could look anywhere in the classroom.
Jack:	We could look on the schedule.
Teacher:	Yes, wherever you want.
Arianna:	So, like if I find *snow*.

Teacher: Yes, great example. Okay, so if you find *snow*—
does the -ow sound like *ou* or *o*?

Arianna: *o.*

Teacher: Okay, so then it goes over here. (*points to the first
column on her paper*)

Jonathan: I just thought of a word, *power.*

Teacher: Fantastic! Does *power* go with *o* or *ou*?

Jonathan: *ou.*

Teacher: Great. Go get started.

Names JONATHAN, JUST, IN Date _____

WORD HUNT

Go on a hunt for words that have __OU__ in
them. Look in books, on posters and
around the room. Do your best to read
the word and put it in the right box.

Sounds like "O"	Sounds like "OU"
Growing	flower
Yellow	How
Low	Wow
Snow	Plow
Know	Brown
pilow	
tomorrow	

FIGURE 2–2: Students Go on a Word Hunt

3

Setting Up Your Word Study Workshop

∫o, you are all ready to incorporate your word study program into your literacy block. You've planned out your minilessons, you have a few inquiries to investigate, and you are ready to introduce the workshop to your students. Of course every classroom, every teacher, and every class of students is different, but I find when you start with a goal and set expectations for your workshop you can always adjust to meet the needs of your particular class. Remember: Reflection and Revision (R and R).

To begin, there are three important factors you may want to consider when preparing to set up your workshop for word study.

- organization
- tone
- independence

Although word study workshop may only take up about twenty minutes of your day, it should be a valuable experience. Either the children can use all twenty minutes to practice their learning or they can use the whole twenty minutes to get organized, ask questions, or disturb others. The setup of your workshop, at the very beginning, will determine how effectively the children use their time.

Organization

Just like any area of your classroom, your word study area should be accessible to children. The games and activities are at children's reach and are clearly labeled and organized into baskets or tubs. The children can be shown where these games are in the classroom before starting and can practice finding the correct games by listening for specific titles and going to get the games off the shelf.

FIGURE 3–1: Word Study Center

You may also want to think of a way to send the children off to play their activities. I recommend keeping a chart of "game assignments," which has many advantages. First, it helps you to send the class off to their assignments quickly and smoothly. Second, when children forget what game they are to play (and this seems to *always* happen, no matter how well the children are listening) you have an easy way of looking it up on your list. And third, the chart will help you keep track of what inquiries the children were practicing for the week and where they should go next. (An example of this class chart is shown in Figure 3–2.)

Tone

Although this is a working and playful time for children, the tone of the classroom can still be one of respect and concentration. Of course, this will differ from teacher to teacher. Personally, I

Word Study Workshop

CHILD'S NAME	DATE: 3/5	DATE:	DATE:	DATE:
Ally	S. Blaster			
Andrew	Poem Detect.			
Aomi	Make a Word			
Alina	Smile Words			
Christopher	Fairy T.Bingo			
Drew	Rhyme Bingo			
Gabriel	Make a Word			
Henry	Word Find			
Jonathan	Mag. Letters			
Jordan	S. Blaster			
Julius	Word Find			
Laura	Fairy T. Bingo			
Madison	Word Train			
Matthew	Read. Rabbit			
Nicole	Poem Detect.			
Olivia	Word Train			
Sabastian	Rhyme Bingo			
Samantha	Smile Words			
Tyler	Mag. Letters			
Victoria	Rhyme Bingo			
Zack	Read. Rabbit			

Inquiry of the week: -en words

Goals: recognize and find the -en spelling pattern in our poems, big books, and their own reading.

Observations:

FIGURE 3–2: Word Study Workshop

cannot concentrate when there is too much noise. I get distracted and aggravated. You can imagine the trouble I sometimes have working in a school in New York City. But I've learned to increase my tolerance for sound and the children have learned to adjust their noise level to accommodate me as well. Not every teacher (or child) has trouble concentrating in a noisy or "lively" classroom. In fact, I have visited many rooms in which the children are all happily on task, the teacher is working with a small group of children, and *I* am losing my mind. What's important is to find your own tolerance level and ensure that all the children are comfortable with it. Some children have a very difficult time in a busy, energized environment. Their needs can be met by finding more isolating games for them—such as the computer or listening center—and by encouraging the other children to respect their distinctiveness.

Once you've found a tone that you and the students are comfortable with, you can practice with the class. If children understand why they need to meet the specific expectations, they can monitor themselves and rise to the occasion. (For example: "We are using quiet voices because everyone needs to be able to concentrate and work to get smarter today." Or, "We will limit the number of times we get out of our seat and move around the room because it is distracting to those of us who are having trouble focusing on our work.")

When the children are held responsible for their own noise monitoring, they are more likely to hear what *we* hear. They begin to listen carefully for irritating noises such as pencil tapping, children running in the halls, chairs squeaking, and so on. But again, this is all relative to what tone is set for your word study workshop. Regardless, young children can be made aware of how they affect those around them and be responsible for the tone and noise level of their group.

Independence

This is probably the most important factor of all three when considering an effective word study workshop. Because of this, I have separated this section into four areas:

1. **HOW TO PLAY THE GAMES:** If the children have not yet learned how to play their word study games, they cannot be expected to remain on task. As new inquiries are taught and as the year progresses, the children are taught new workshop games. Most often, the game is taught to the entire class at once and then put into the word study center. Sometimes, only a few children are taught a game—maybe as a challenge or special privilege. As new children learn a game, they can be asked to teach it to others. It's important to monitor (or assign) the game and activity selections. Children often want to play games that are either too challenging or too repetitive for them. This usually causes disruption and poor behavior and, most important, is a waste of time.

2. **INTERRUPTIONS AND QUESTIONS:** Young children *always* have plenty of questions and comments throughout their learning. This is usually one of the most enjoyable parts of the day, but it sometimes needs to be saved for specific times. During your workshop time, children can learn to save their

questions and comments (unless crucial) until the end of the workshop and attempt to continue their activity. It can be suggested that they write their questions down, ask a friend for advice, or take a risk to do the best they can with the task(s) at hand. As the teacher, you may want to set ground rules to avoid such questions as, "May I go to the bathroom?" or "May I get a drink?" or "May I play a different game?" As long as the entire class knows what to do in any of the above situations, the questions can be avoided in the future.

3. **PROBLEM SOLVING:** Sometimes children come across problems while they are playing their games. These problems can range anywhere from running out of worksheets for one of the games to a pair of children arguing about whose turn it is next. In order to avoid becoming the police officer in the room instead of the teacher, I suggest that the class talk about some of these problems before going off to play. You can role model typical situations or simply discuss them as they come up. Once addressed, the class should know how to problem solve in that area and not need to interrupt anyone over these issues. Some common solutions to these problems can be as simple as playing another game, asking a third party to make a decision, or cleaning up the game and taking out a book to read (if no other solution seems to work out). Although you will be monitoring the class and observing the children, you will want to be helping to keep the children on task and making the most of their learning—*not* making decisions about which child "goes next."

4. **WHAT TO DO WHEN YOU'RE DONE:** Children work at different paces and need to be aware of what they can do when they finish early. This was always a big challenge for me as a new teacher. Everyone would be working quietly and with great enthusiasm. Then three excitable children would finish early. They would start wrestling on the rug and the entire class would lose its harmony. It was so upsetting. Once I learned to establish other assignments for children who are done early, not only did the class remain intact but the children tended to spend more time on their original assignment. When the workshop comes to an end, children need to know how to clean up their games properly and where to put them away so that others will be able to find them the next day. Also, if students are working on worksheets they will need to know what to do with them when they are through. This decision will be personal to each teacher—Will the children bring this work home? Will they have word study folders to keep their work in? Either way, this decision should be consistent and pertain to all children in the class.

FIGURE 3–3: One Child Helping Another

4

Motivation
Making Word Study Fun for Young Children

We all know that children are going to be more successful learners if they have fun while they work. Some of the most precious moments in my teaching career have been when my students break out in a cheer upon being told that it's time for read-aloud. Or when they sigh sadly after being told that word study workshop is over and it's time to clean up. I was one of those lucky ones when I was little; I loved being in school and I was enthusiastic about everything my teacher said. Unfortunately, for most children this is not the case, and we are challenged to excite, interest, and motivate *all* our students. Of course not *every* student is going to be enthusiastic about *all* our lessons but we must try hard to make their learning fun and help them to feel active in their own understanding.

Although not everyone would agree, studying words and how they work is exciting. Children are just learning to read and to notice similarities in our language. Their eyes light up when they recognize a word or find a spelling pattern that they just learned. It's fun to hunt for words, chant words that rhyme, make new discoveries about sounds in words, and create a rule that's going to help you spell a word correctly. We, as teachers, can guide children to make these connections at every possible moment—to shout them out as we see them and reward children when they learn something new.

There are many ways to motivate children to learn. I find that being a positive, reflective teacher and allowing children to be involved in the learning can really stimulate my classroom. During word study I like to begin my lessons by explaining what we are going to be focusing on and why I have chosen that specific inquiry to study. This helps the children understand the purpose for their learning and reminds them of previous lessons and activities. Also, I make sure to have students work either together as a whole class or with one or two others, in small groups.

On the next few pages I include some sample lessons for word study. Each study focuses on a different inquiry—from a fairly common spelling pattern to a more complicated study on apostrophes. Each lesson builds on the previous day's and every student is given the opportunity to investigate and make new discoveries. In all instances, the students are motivated by the teacher's explanation of the lesson and by their interaction with each other.

Sample Weekly Schedules

Because much of the focus in the lower grades is on spelling patterns, the following two schedules focus on the use of a high-frequency word to learn a new spelling pattern. The charts in Figures 4–1 and 4–2 represent a typical weekly schedule, including the focus for the day, the minilesson to introduce it, the student's participation, and the extension activities. Although not all inquiries are taught in exactly this way, much of our word study learning fits into this model.

The chart in Figure 4–3 represents a typical weekly schedule but differs a bit from the previous two. It still includes the focus for the day, the minilesson to introduce it, the student's participation, and the extension activities, but much of the work is done with either the whole class or in partnerships.

A Sample of an Intermediate Word Study Lesson

TEACHER FOCUS: *A review of words that have the -en spelling pattern.*

Teacher: We've spent most of the week talking about the word *when* and how it can help us spell many other words. When I call your name, please go get a wipe-off board, a marker, and a cloth and sit in a circle on the rug.

(As the class prepares, the children sit next to someone who has a different-color marker than they do. They have played this game before and know exactly how to set up. The different-color marker is used as a highlighter.)

Teacher: Okay, when you're ready, write the word *when* right in the center of your board. Let's snap it quickly in case we forgot how to spell it.

Sample Weekly Schedule for Word Study/Grades K–1

DAY	FOCUS	MINILESSON	STUDENT INTERACTION	WORKSHOP ACTIVITIES
1	Reviewing the word *went* as a high-frequency word.	I notice the class using the word *went* in their reading and writing a lot. You use it when you write "I went to my friends house" or "We went on a class trip." Let's make sure that we all know how to spell *went* correctly.	The class "snaps out" the word *went*: "W-E-N-T . . . WENT!" Three or four students may come up to the front of the class. One frames the word in a big book displayed on the easel, one spells it with magnetic letters on the board, and one may write it on a wipe-off board. In the meantime, the rest of the class may spell it with their finger in the air or on the rug in front of them.	Children may be involved in many different activities: • Word Wall Bingo • Sight Word Bingo • Make It and Break It • Word Wall Word Find • Word Detective
2	Recognizing that *went* has the -ent spelling pattern.	Yesterday we reviewed the word *went* as a word we use a lot. *Went* is a great word to know because it helps us spell many other words. Can anyone think of other words that sound like *went*?	As the children offer new words that they know, I can write the words on a chart tablet, high-lighting the spelling pattern -ent.	The children use playdough, magnetic letters, wipe-off boards, and alphabet cubes to first try and spell *went* and then some of the words that that sound like *went*.
3	Learning how to spell other words using *went* as the base word.	Now that we know a lot of words that sound like *went*, let's try and spell some of those words. If we know how to spell *went*, then we know how to spell *tent* or *sent*. Who can come up and spell a new word using the -ent spelling pattern?	I already have a magnetic board out with the letters E N T at the top. The consonant letters that the children will need to spell their list of words from yesterday should be on the bottom of the board. As each child comes up to spell a new word the class can snap out the word: "T-E-N-T . . . TENT!"	Most of the children in the class are involved in games and activities that help them to practice using the new spelling pattern: • Make a Word • Word Detective • Smile Words • Spelling Pattern Game • Stamp It Out • Spelling Pattern Detective • Word Train • Word Search

| 4 | Practicing the spelling of words that have the -ent spelling pattern. | I took all the magnetic letters that we used yesterday and put them here on the overhead projector. Who can walk up to the screen and point to the letter that would help me spell *sent*? | As the class looks up at the large screen in front of them, one child may walk over and point to the *S* on the bottom of the screen. The rest of the class confirms that this was the correct letter to spell *sent*, as I move the letter to the top of the screen, putting it together with -ent. I continue calling children up to spell other -ent words. | Yesterday's games can be rotated. Each child should be matched to an appropriate game—choosing the right level of challenge for each individual student. |
| 5 | Recording our learning for future practice. | Using all the words that you spelled with magnetic letters yesterday, we are going to practice writing our -ent words today. Please snap out and then write the word *went* in the middle of your wipe-off board. Put a box around the spelling pattern -ent. That part is going to stay the same. | As each child writes the word *went* in the middle of their boards, I can call on children to suggest a new word to write. The class erases the *W* (from *went*) and puts the letter that they think will help them to spell the new word. The class looks around at their classmates' boards and at my board for confirmation. The activity is continued until the class can no longer think of new words to write. Before erasing the entire board, the children should always go back to the focus word, *went*, and write it one last time. | Some of the children are handed an index card with one of the -ent words on it (the spelling pattern is highlighted). As some children are called on to shout out a word that sounds like *went*, the others must look in their hands to see if they are holding it. As each child's word is called, they may come up and put the word in the hanging pocket chart underneath the word *went*. The word *went* goes on the word wall with a smiley face (or star) in the corner. This will remind the students that it can help them to spell other words. |

FIGURE 4-1: Sample Weekly Schedule for Word Study/Grades K–1

Sample Weekly Schedule for Word Study/Grade 2

DAY	FOCUS	MINILESSON	STUDENT INTERACTION	WORKSHOP ACTIVITIES
1	Reviewing the word *night* as a high-frequency word.	I notice the class using the word *night* in their reading and writing a lot. Today we are going to read a book together called *It Didn't Frighten Me* by Janet Goss. After reading the story we are going to look at the word *night* to make sure that we all know how to spell it correctly.	The class will watch as I write the word *night* on the board. The children will look closely at the word and name each letter aloud. As I cover up the word, the children will all attempt to write it on their wipe-off boards (or in notebooks or on clipboards). When done, they will check their spelling and correct any mistakes.	Children may be involved in many different activities: • Word Wall Bingo • Sight Word Bingo • Making Words • Sound Hunt • Make Your Own Word Find • Word Wall Word Find
2	Recognizing that *night* has the -ight spelling pattern.	Today we are going to reread *It Didn't Frighten Me* but this time we are going to listen for other words that sound like *night*. We will create a web of all the words that we hear.	I write *night* on a chart. As the class hears words that sound like *night*, they can begin to volunteer words to add to web.	The class will partner up and play Spelling Pattern Detective. They will share their findings with the class.
3	Learning how to build on other words by already knowing how to spell *night*.	As a class, we are going to build upon the words that you found yesterday with the -ight spelling pattern. How do you think knowing the word *night* will help you become a better speller? What other words are you now able to spell?	The class will review the web of -ight words and use their detective sheets from the previous day to add on to their lists of words. They will attempt to spell words such as: *flashlight, nighttime, frightening,* etc. . . .	Most of the children will play a version of Word Detective. They will take their list of words and look in books and magazines for words with -ight in them. They will record if the spelling pattern comes at the beginning of the word (*lightening*), the middle of the word (*heighten*), or at the end of the word (*daylight*). Other children may be playing: • Make a Word (more review) • Word Sort (challenge)

4	Practicing spelling words that have the -ight spelling pattern.	During Interactive Writing today we are all going to have a chance at practicing our spelling of words with the -ight spelling pattern.	I will tell a story using four or five words with -ight in it. (Ex: "Last night I had to walk up six flights of stairs. It was nighttime and it was hard to set sight on each step. What a delight it was to finally get home.") The children will take turns writing the sentences on the board while the others write on their wipe-off boards.	The students will work in pairs to try and come up with a story on their own using at least three words with -ight in them. Other children may be playing: • Make Your Own Word Find • Word Detective (from yesterday) • Smile Words
5	Assessing our learning for future understanding.	To make sure that everyone is now an "expert" on -ight words, we are going to have a dictation. I am going to give you a sentence using words with -ight in them, and you are going to do your best to write the sentence and spell the words correctly.	I give the dictation: "The light burns brightly at night." The children are reminded to think about the words that the class has worked on all week and do the best they can to write the sentence.	For last review the entire class can be engaged in a number of different activities: • Spelling Pattern Detective • Word Train • Word Sort • Make a Word • Make Your Own Word Find • Smile Words • Stamp It Out

FIGURE 4–2: Sample Weekly Schedule for Word Study/Grade 2

Sample Weekly Schedule for Word Study/Grade 3

DAY	FOCUS	MINILESSON	STUDENT INTERACTION	WORKSHOP ACTIVITIES
1	Looking at apostrophes and what they do.	Many words are spelled with apostrophes. Today, I am going to read you a poem. At first, I just ask you that you listen to the poem. When I'm through, I'll read it again and put it up on the overhead screen for you to see.	The students listen to the poem to get a feel for the content. After I put it on the screen and read it again, the students are asked to search the poem and write down all the words they see that have an apostrophe.	The students work in small groups (two to three members in each) to compare their lists of words and see if they missed any. They will be asked to begin looking at the words and discuss why these words had an apostrophe in them.
2	Learning the reasons for an apostrophe.	Yesterday we all looked at a poem and noticed that many words had apostrophes in them for different reasons. (Probably the students noticed that they were used to show possessives and contractions.) Today, I'd like to read you a couple of pages from the book *Minty: A Story of Young Harriet Tubman*, by Alan Schroeder. When I'm done, I'll put a few more pages on the overhead. (The teacher may want to make sure to already have read this book once prior to the lesson or make sure to read it again, from the beginning.)	The students volunteer to read the remaining pages out loud to their classmates. When they are done, they will take out their lists of words from yesterday and add any new ones they may have seen today.	The students get into their groups from yesterday and revisit their lists of words with apostrophes. They may notice new reasons for using an apostrophe (to show dialect, for example) and discuss these reasons as a group.

3	Recognizing words with apostrophes by hearing them.	Over the past two days we have looked at passages that contained words with apostrophes. You've done a great job formulating rules and reasons for the use of an apostrophe. Today, we are going to play a game. In this game you must LISTEN for words that have apostrophes. You won't see the word so you must listen carefully. I will model it for you before sending you away to play.	One or two students are chosen to join me in the game. I pull out stacks of index cards with sentences already written on them. As the students listen to one sentence at a time, they must write down the word they heard that had an apostrophe in it. If they get the word right, they get one point. If they also spell it correctly, they receive two points.	The students play the game in groups of three. They take turns reading the cards and writing their answers on their paper. At the end of the game, the students can total up their points and assess their understanding.
4	Practicing spelling words with apostrophes.	I noticed that you all won many points in the game yesterday but still need some more practice with spelling words with apostrophes. We are going to have a Shared Writing lesson today in which we will attempt to write from a slave's point of view, hiding on the Underground Railroad. She is writing in her diary . . .	After I have set up the scenario and written the opening sentence, the students are asked to come up and add on to the story, trying their best to include many words with apostrophes in them.	The students can either copy down the class' story in their spelling notebook/folder or rewrite their own, using words with apostrophes. (Some of these words may be used as the class' spelling words in the future.)
5	Assessing our learning for future understanding.	To better analyze how the class has understood our work on apostrophes, I am going to give you a dictation that I want you all to try your best on and write down exactly what I say.	The students listen to me dictate the passage and write down what they hear.	Before handing in their dictations, students can assess their own learning by analyzing their papers and writing a brief note to the teacher about what they feel confident about or what they need more work on.

FIGURE 4–3: Sample Weekly Schedule for Word Study/Grade 3

Class:	W-H-E-N . . . WHEN!
Teacher:	Trade markers with someone next to you to high-light the part of the word that's going to stay the same. Draw a box around -en.
Teacher:	Great. Justin, you made a box around the entire word *when*. Just box the part of the word that's going to stay on your board the whole time. We are going to erase the *w* and the *h* to make new words. Good, you got it. Now, get ready to erase the *wh*—who can think of a word that sounds like *when*?
Erica:	*Ten*.
Teacher:	Great! What letter should we put up on our boards?
Erica:	A *t*.
Teacher:	What does it say?
Class:	*Ten*!
Teacher:	Who else?
Jack:	*Then—th-*.
Teacher.	Th . . . *then*. Good. Erase the *th-* and let's write . . .
Jonathan:	*Blend*.
Teacher:	*Blend*. Great! Now let's be careful. What should we start with?
Jonathan:	Bl.
Teacher:	Put the *bl-* in front of the box with -en. Now what?
Lily:	Put a *d* on the other side of the box.
Teacher:	Good, everyone put a *d* at the end of the word. *Bl* . . . *en* . . . *d*.
Joe:	*Men*.
Teacher:	What letter?
Joe:	*M*.
David:	*Jen*.
Teacher:	Great, David. What should we write?
David:	*J*.
Teacher:	That's right. But *Jen* is a name so let's be sure to write an uppercase *J*.

Yuri:	*Hungry.*
Teacher:	Yuri . . . *men, ten, then, Jen* . . .
Arianna:	No, she said *Henry.*
Teacher:	Oh! (*laughs*) Sorry, Yuri, I thought you said *hungry!* (*Everyone laughs.*) Yes, *Henry!* Good. What should we write?
Yuri:	*H?*
Teacher:	Good, Yuri. Let's put a capital *H* because it's a name.
Lily:	That's my brother's name!
Teacher:	Oh, great! Do you want to help us spell it? What do we do after the *H*?
Lily:	You have to put an *r* and a *y* at the end. Like this. (*writes it on her board and shows the class*)
	(*The class goes through a few more words, continuing to erase and write new ones. In the meantime, the teacher has written all the words on index cards as the children come up with them. Each word is written in one color but the -en is boxed with another color.*)
Teacher:	Let's go back to the word we started with. Put up wh-. What does your board say?
Class:	*When!*
Teacher:	Great. Snap it out.
Class:	W-H-E-N . . . WHEN!
Teacher:	Okay, erase your boards but leave them right where they are. I'm going to hand out our cards with -en words. Remember, not everyone always gets a card but everyone can help call out the words.
Mariah:	*Pen.*
Teacher:	Who's holding the card with *pen* on it?
Takuma:	I am!
Teacher:	Great, come on up.
	(*Takuma hands the teacher his index card and the teacher puts it in a pocket chart beneath the word* when. *These cards will remain in the pocket chart*

until a new word is studied. When they are removed, they are made into a book and hung near the word wall under the word when*.*)

Teacher: Who wants to call out another word?

Elie: *Then!*

Teacher: Who has *then*?

Max: Me!

Teacher: Come on up Max and put it in the chart.

(*The class continues until all cards are collected.*)

Teacher: Look at all the words you know just from learning *when*! Wow, that's exciting. From now on, if you hear a word that sounds like *when*, you will know how to spell it! Okay, please clean up your boards and markers and come back to the rug for read-aloud.

FIGURE 4–4: Our Spelling Pattern Chart.

FIGURE 4–5: Highlighting Spelling Patterns

5

What Is Assessment?

*A*ssessment can be seen as a photograph of your students' learning. Although there are many different kinds of assessments, they all serve one purpose: to take a picture of your class' understanding and evaluate the success of your teaching.

Assessments can be given at various times throughout the year. You may want to assess the children's knowledge before teaching a specific inquiry to better prepare your lessons. Assessing mid-inquiry helps you to know where to go next and assessing at the end of each study will assist in planning for future lessons.

Organizing and participating in assessments is easy. Evaluating them and using them for more effective teaching is hard. Because of this, you must use an assessment that makes sense to you. There are formal and informal assessments—both are equally valuable. I have included some different examples of assessments that I have found helpful. It's a good idea to try different ones and see which give you the most information about your class. Also, some are useful for specific purposes and may be given only at particular times or to particular children.

Due to the variety of assessments, you must beware of the constant battle between busywork and assessment. I have found myself spending way too much time filling out assessments and organizing them into fancy binders with color coding, and so on. It's good to be organized, yes. But if you are not going back to these papers and using them on a daily basis for your planning, then it is simply a waste of time. Fancy binders with color-coded dividers can only be celebrated if they're being used. Although some formal assessments are completed and looked at momentarily before being placed in permanent portfolios or folders, informal ones should be at your fingertips at all times. Many children learn at unbelievable speeds and modify their understanding on a daily basis. We need to keep track of this learning and continue to take "pictures" of it as often as possible.

What does all this mean in reference to word study? We are asking children to take information about words they've learned and transfer this knowledge to their independent work. We expect them to become fluent, confident readers and spellers. But how can we expect this from them if we can never be sure of how much they understand? Looking at children's spelling and listening to them read will help us to be more aware of what they already know and what they still struggle with.

Making Meaning from Assessments

We can use assessments to look for the following behaviors:

- Are they noticing spelling patterns inside words and using them to read or spell an unknown word? For example: -est in the word *best*.

- Are they looking for or listening for familiar chunks of words? (Are they recognizing a familiar blend, digraph, or suffix?) For example: tr- and -er in *trainer*.

- Are they noticing base words inside of larger words? For example: quickly seeing the word *part* inside *apartment*.

- Are they using words that they already know to help them spell a new word? For example: "If I already know how to spell *pail* then I can spell *sail*. And if I know how to spell *or* than I can spell *sailor*."

On the other hand, asking children to be able to perform the above behaviors, we assume that they understand how to put words together and break them apart. We are also assuming that they can hear the similarities in words. But what if they are unable to master any of these skills? Using appropriate assessments will help us work with children and modify our expectations of them. After reading *The Phonological Awareness Handbook for Kindergarten and Primary Teachers* by Lita Ericson and Moira Fraser Juliebo, I have taken some of the suggested assessments for children who struggle with blending and segmenting sounds and who have difficulty hearing rhyming words. I adjusted the assessments to better meet the needs of my students—classroom populations vary and assessments can reflect these changes. (Only informal assessments should be modified to meet the needs of the classroom students. Formal assessments are based on benchmarks and need to remain true to their foundation.) Examples of these modified assessments are listed in Appendixes B, C, and D.

After performing one of these three modified assessment tests, I may find that a few of my students are still struggling with phonemic awareness and need continued support in this area. Although I would not remove them from the class' group lessons, I would make sure to choose appropriate games and activities during word study workshop (see Chapter 6, "Activities for Beginning Readers") and would work with a small, guided, word study group in any of the needed areas.

There have been times when no assessment is able to meet the needs of a particular purpose of mine. In this case, I have chosen to make up my own. This is a great learning experience and I suggest that anyone who has not yet tried it think of a particular area of teaching where you feel least confident and create an assessment for the children to evaluate your success rate. You will be greatly pleased at the results! (Or incredibly surprised— in which case, aren't you glad you discovered this?)

As my school began to reevaluate our word study program, I decided to create an assessment that would help me have access to my students' understanding of the inquiries I had taught. I made a list of all our word study minilessons. Then I created a list of words that incorporated a little bit of all the inquiries— coming up with a list of fourteen words. I worked with small groups so the children felt less intimidated. I gave each student in the group a piece of paper with fourteen blank lines on it. I called out the words on my list, reading them slowly and creating a sentence for each. The students worked one by one to try and spell the word I had called out. In the meantime, the other students were working on assigned word study games and activities. When the entire class was assessed, I collected all the papers and put their results into a chart. In this way, I was able to get a cross section of their learning and have access to the results on only one piece of paper. From the assessment, I was able to evaluate my lessons, prepare future minilessons, plan small, guided, word study groups, and better understand where to go next with my word study program.

Figure 5–1 shows a few results of a word study assessment test given midyear to a kindergarten class. The organization of this chart helped me get an overview of the class. Although many children will learn strategies for spelling and comprehend the purpose of word study instruction, they do not all transfer their understanding to their independent work. In isolation, a young child may master an activity focused on -ice words, for example, but when asked, out of context, to write a word that has the -ice sound, she may not recognize the learned spelling pattern (see Madison's attempt to spell *price*).

While using the chart for assessment purposes to plan for individual, small-group and whole-class instruction, it is important

Assessment for Word Study: A Class Cross Section

	PANDA	WINDOW	RIDDLE	FORGOT	PLUG	CHILLY	HANDLE	PRICE	CHATTER	STAY	MITTEN	DROP	CALLED	SPELLING
Jordan	panda	window	redel	forgot	plog	chile	handil	priyes	chader	stay	metten	drop	called	spelling
Henry	pand	windo	ridul	fergot	plug	chiley	handul	pruys	chatuer	stay	mitin	drop	calld	speling
Tyler	panda	windo	ratl	forgt	plag	chilly	handll	pris	chatr	sta	mtin	drp	clld	spling
Sam	panda	window	ridel	forgot	plug	chily	handel	price	chader	sta	mitin	drop	called	spelling
Nicole	pada	wido	ritall	forgit	paug	cly	hdall	pirs	chadr	staya	mitine	dip	cide	spling
Jon	pandu	window	widel	fugut	plug	chiley	hadonl	pws	chader	stay	mitin	dwop	cud	speling
Andrew	panda	windo	ridul	furgot	pluge	chily	handule	price	chadre	stay	miten	droppe	called	spaling
Aomi	pennda	window	ridel	forgot	plug	chillye	handole	price	cheater	stay	mitten	drop	called	spelling
Madison	panda	window	ritle	forgot	plug	chilly	handle	pris	chater	stay	mitin	grop	called	speling

FIGURE 5–1: Nine Students' Spelling Attempts

to look for patterns or trends in the students' progress. Are most of the children in the class failing to recognize the -en spelling pattern? Are a few children struggling with short vowel sounds? These are some questions to look for while assessing the class results, and it is these specific inquiries that will guide a teacher's word study planning. When the majority of the class needs more instruction in a specific area, the inquiry should be revisited. If only a few children need more work, a small group can be pulled for guided instruction during word study workshop.

Some Common Confusions and Suggestions for Correction

1. Child is leaving out strong consonant sounds. (See Nicole's attempt to spell *window*.)

   Suggestion: Ask child to reread word back to you just as it is written.

2. Child is not hearing all sounds in the word. (See Tyler's attempt to spell *forgot*.)

   Suggestion: Work with the student on stretching out words—listening for more sounds. Rubber bands serve as great "word stretchers," and wipe-off boards can be used to record the sounds the child hears.

3. Child is not recognizing common spelling patterns in words. (See Andrew's attempt to spell *drop*.)

   Suggestion: The student should spend more time working with learned spelling patterns. He can come up with lists of words that have the same spelling pattern (starting with one he already knows and moving toward more challenging ones). Constant repetition and play with spelling pattern games and activities are always good reinforcements.

4. Child is not recognizing common word endings. (See Henry's attempt to spell *called*.)

   Suggestion: Set student up with a partner or small group to chart words with the same endings, looking for patterns in the spelling of the words. The students should analyze their findings and come up with a list of spelling rules on their own.

5. Child is confusing vowel letters and sounds. (See Jordan's attempt to spell *plug*.)

   Suggestion: The student should play many word sorting games, focusing on words with short vowel sounds. The student can sort the words by what vowel they possess.

Always ask a child why they spelled a word the way they did. Their answer may tell you more about what kind of speller they are than any assessment test!

6

Activities for Beginning Readers

$\mathcal{U}$sing children's names for word study is the most appropriate and most enjoyable learning experience for struggling children. Here are some basic ideas for either whole-class or small-group activities:

● Clap out each child's name so that they hear the number of syllables in each name. Have the class guess whose name you are clapping out by training them to listen for the number of claps (and how each name "sounds").

● Have students use foam or magnetic letters to match the letters in their name (written out on a large card) with their classmates' names.

● Write every child's name on a sentence strip. Sort the names on the carpet based on the lengths of the names. Have the children guess how you have sorted them. Encourage them to look at the lengths of the words—count the letters in each name. Chart who has the longest and the shortest name in the class (Cunningham and Allington 1994).

● Turn the name strips over and put two down in front of you. Give the class two choices of names and ask them to figure out which name is which, based on the length of the strip. For example: "One of these name strips says Alexandra and the other says Mike. Can you guess which is which without turning them over?" (Cunningham and Allington 1994).

● Sort the class' names by their first letters, looking at how many children start with an *A*, how many with a *G*, etc . . .

● Play Name Bingo with the class, highlighting the first letters of their names on the boards to concentrate on using the first letter for help. (In Name Bingo, the children's boards are covered with student names instead of numbers or letters.)

● Read tons of alphabet books, calling out all the things that start with the same first letters as children's names.

● Make a book of things that start with the same letter as each child's name. For example: *Buttons* start like *Ben*. *Jackets* start like *Julie*. Take photos of the objects in the room.

● Have children bring in foods that start with the same letter as their name and have an alphabet party.

Recognizing the alphabet and helping children become familiar with and confident in their knowledge of letters and sounds is crucial to their basic phonemic awareness. Here are some suggestions for games, activities, and learning experiences that will help them become more fluent with the alphabet:

● Play any version of alphabet bingo—starting with ones that have pictures included on the cards and boards.

● Play I Spy with the alphabet chart in your room. For example: "I spy a letter on the chart that starts the word *flower*." Or, "I spy a picture on the chart that starts the same as *tiger*."

● Have the child (or children) make their own alphabet book—either drawing pictures or cutting out photos from magazines. Encourage them to practice writing the letter that the picture starts with. Bind the book for them and help them celebrate their work.

● Listen to alphabet stories in the listening center.

● Hide magnetic letters in socks and have the child guess what the letter is by the feel of its shape.

● Use magnetic letters to match up with alphabet cards, choosing a card with a picture on it and finding the magnetic letter that goes with the first letter of the word.

● Have a child trace over dark, enlarged letters with glue and sand. When the glue dries, ask the child to practice tracing the letters with her fingers to get the "feel" of what it looks like.

● Have children use playdough to make letters or spell sight words they are learning. Creating the shape of the letters will help them think about the form of the letter.

● Play memory with alphabet picture cards. Turn the cards over so only the picture side is showing. Find a match of two cards that have pictures of things that start with the same letter. Turn

FIGURE 6–1: Playing the Sock Game

FIGURE 6–2: Spelling Words with Playdough

the cards over to reveal the "answers" (alphabet letters) on the underside of the card.

● Use alphabet jigsaw puzzles with large pieces (one letter per piece) to help the children sequence the alphabet—finding the "next piece" or next letter of the alphabet.

● *When using an alphabet chart as a source of reference, be consistent!* Use the same chart each time you need to refer to one. You can also send a copy of the chart home for the family to use.

Listening for rhyming words and letter combinations that sound the same is a difficult task for some struggling students. Here are some suggestions for games, activities, and learning experiences that will help children hear commonalities in words:

● Play any version of Rhyming Bingo. Give the students boards with words on it and call out ones that would rhyme. Start with very basic rhyming words such as: *bat/cat* and *man/can*. Then move on to a more sophisticated version: *down/clown* or *skate/ plate*.

● Work with a small group, cutting out pictures of objects from magazines or workbooks that rhyme with objects you hold on up on index cards. As each student finds a picture, they can glue it onto the back of the index card.

● Make a memory game using pictures of objects. Make sure that each object has a match that rhymes with it. Have the children flip over cards looking for an object that sounds like the one they have already found.

● Listen to Dr. Seuss stories in the listening center.

● Read many rhyming books aloud to the class. Challenge the class by pausing just before the second verse of the rhyme, allowing the children to try and guess the word. (For example: "He went to bed and turned off the light. He gave mommy a kiss and said 'Good _____.' ")

● Play I Spy with an alphabet chart in the room; make it into a rhyming game. For example: "I spy a picture on our alphabet chart that starts with an *h* and sounds like *mouse*."

● Prepare pages of pictures with many objects that rhyme and one or two that do not rhyme. Work with the children, saying the names of the objects aloud, listening for the ones that sound the same, and crossing off the ones that do not.

7

Using Poetry to Have Fun with Word Study

*P*oetry is a very large part of my classroom learning. We use poems for shared reading, for theme work, for illustration projects, for writing workshop, and for word study. The variations of poems you use and how often you introduce a new one depends on the classroom's particular needs and the style of the teacher. Although some poems are not always of huge interest to the children, they may be used for specific and quick minilessons, while others may be appreciated all week long.

When working with poems, the teacher can copy them on a piece of chart paper and hang it in front of the class, put the poem on an overhead projector and project it onto a screen, photocopy individual sheets for children, or do all three. However you present them, poems are great for word study. Most often, it's easy to find rhyming words, repetition of common spelling patterns, word endings, blends, digraphs, contractions, homophones, and compound words. (See Appendix H for samples of poems.) On some occasions it is difficult to find a poem that includes the specific word study inquiry your class is working on. In this case, I recommend attempting your own poem. It can be challenging and probably won't be your best piece of writing, but it will be a useful teaching tool for two reasons:

1. You can incorporate any inquiry you desire.

2. Your students have the opportunity to see you as a writer. This serves as a wonderful model for them. (You can have older students write their own poem as part of the word study workshop. This can be a whole-class or small-group activity.)

Games and Activities for Working with Poems

● Enlarge a poem on an overhead projector and ask children to come up and circle specific word study inquiries. (You can use markers made for overhead projectors that will wash off after use.)

● Enlarge a poem on an overhead projector after cutting out (or covering up) special words (ones of interest to your study). Have children come up and fill in the missing words.

● Play I Spy with a poem. For example: "I spy a word that starts with an *r*. It has four letters and sounds like *main*." Children can either come up in front of the class and point to the word on a chart or circle it on their individual copy of the poem.

● Children can work in partnerships or small groups, searching for specific spelling patterns, homophones, contractions, etc., on their own copies of class poems. They can circle what they have found and come back to share with the class.

● Children can work with a partner to find words that rhyme within a poem. They can circle the words, make lists of their findings, or highlight them with markers.

● Play with sight words. Make copies of the poems but leave out the sight words that the class is learning. The children can fill in the words with a pencil. For a different way to play this activity, have the words on small cards and ask the children to Velcro the correct sight words in the appropriate spots.

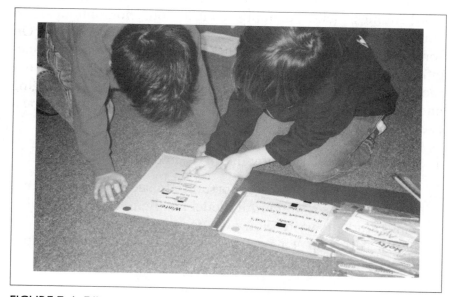

FIGURE 7–1: Filling in Missing Sight Words

Homework: Please practice reading our poem with someone at home and then draw a picture to match the words. Bring this poem back to school tomorrow.

SCHOOL

School is great because
We all learn together.
Making friends
Forever and ever.
We can share, read, have fun.
Working harder
Until the year is done!

-By Lauren Berman & K-211 (2002)

Name Kaede

FIGURE 7–2: A student illustrates the weekly poem.

● Record the class reading the poem and put it in the listening center with a book of all the poems the class has already learned. The students can listen to the poems as they practice reading along.

● For homework, have the children bring home a copy of the poem. They can practice reading it with an adult and then draw a matching picture. All the poems can be collected and stored in poetry folders. The children can use these folders as references for future word study learning.

Games and Activities for Word Study

TITLE: The Sock Game

PURPOSE: To help students recognize and name the letters in the alphabet. (Also, they will become more familiar with the class alphabet chart and the pictures that correspond with each letter.)

MATERIALS NEEDED:

- The Sock Game worksheet (Figure 8–1)
- pencils
- a pair of socks
- magnetic letters (large)
- class alphabet chart
- crayons or markers
- blindfold or scarf

PREPARATION AND STORAGE:

1. Make several photocopies of the game worksheet and keep them in a folder with one copy on the cover so children know what's inside.

2. Decide if you want the students to play with all the magnetic letters or pick out a few that they need to become more familiar with.

3. Put the magnetic letters, blindfold, socks, and copies of the alphabet chart in a tub or a Ziplock bag. Label it "The Sock Game."

INSTRUCTIONS:

1. Pair up two children to work together as partners.

2. Give each pair one or two worksheets. (The students can either work on the same piece of paper or take their own.)

3. One student covers her eyes with the blindfold while the other takes a letter to hide in the sock. Once the letter is hidden, the blindfold can come off, but many children like to leave it on for the fun of it.

4. The student with the blindfold must feel through the sock to try and guess what letter is inside. If necessary, his partner can give hints, such as, "It has two straight lines and one curvy line."

5. After three incorrect guesses are made, the students can pull the letter out and see what it is.

6. They must record the letter inside the picture of the sock on their worksheet.

7. Next, they can use the alphabet chart to write a word and draw a picture of something that begins with the hidden letter.

Names _____ & _____

Date _____

The Sock Game

Hide a magnetic letter in the sock and give it to your partner to guess what letter. (No peeking!) After the letter is pulled out, use the alphabet chart to write a word that begins with that letter. You can also draw a picture of something that starts with the same letter.

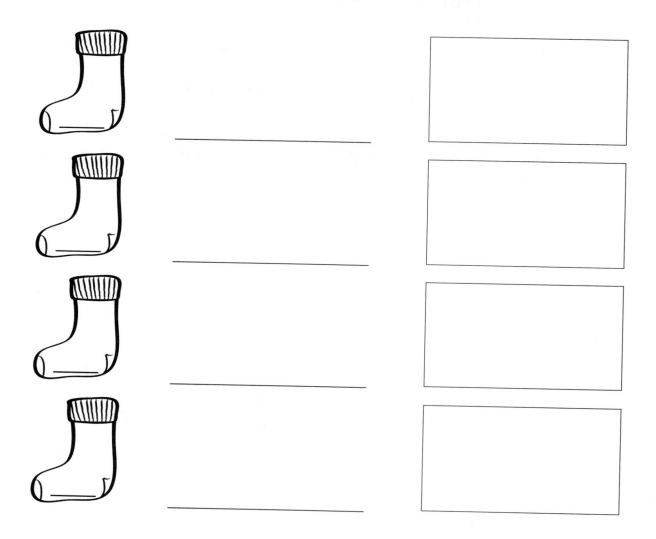

FIGURE 8–1: The Sock Game Worksheet

TITLE: Make a Word

PURPOSE: To familiarize children with specific spelling patterns and the various words they can spell from them.

MATERIALS NEEDED:

- spelling pattern dice
- Make a Word worksheet (Figure 8–3)
- pencils
- Ziplock bag or plastic tub
- folder

PREPARATION AND STORAGE:

1. Find pairs of same-color dice and begin to label your spelling patterns. Use one die for the onsets (beginning consonants of your words) and the other for the spelling pattern. On the first die, write a different letter on all faces of the cube—making sure to choose letters that will form words with your spelling pattern. On the second die, write the spelling pattern on all six faces of the cube.

2. Make a number of photocopies of the worksheet and keep them in a folder with one copy on the cover so children know what's inside.

3. Place all the spelling pattern dice in a Ziplock bag or small plastic tub and label it "Make a Word."

INSTRUCTIONS:

1. Pair two children together to be partners and give them worksheets. Although each child should record on their own sheet, they may roll the same set of spelling pattern dice.

2. Suggest that the children start with a specific spelling pattern (perhaps one the class is studying?) and then may choose their own when they are through.

3. Once a spelling pattern is chosen, the students will write it in the box at the top of the worksheet.

4. The students will take turns rolling the pair of same-color spelling pattern dice. Once the dice are rolled, they will record their rolls on the worksheet.

5. The students will write the letter of the first die in the first box on their paper. They will write the letters of the spelling pattern on the second box on their paper. They

will then put all the letters together and write the full word on the line provided (Figure 8–2).

6. When the students have rolled five times together, they may return the dice to the bag and choose a new set.

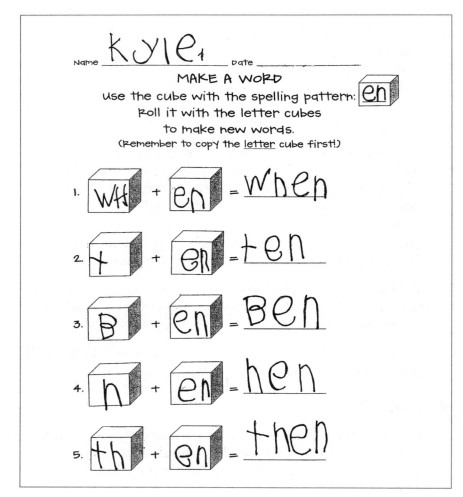

FIGURE 8–2: Make a Word

Name _____

Date _____

Make a Word

Use the cube with the spelling pattern:
Roll it with the letter cubes
to make new words.
(Remember to copy the <u>letter</u> cube first!)

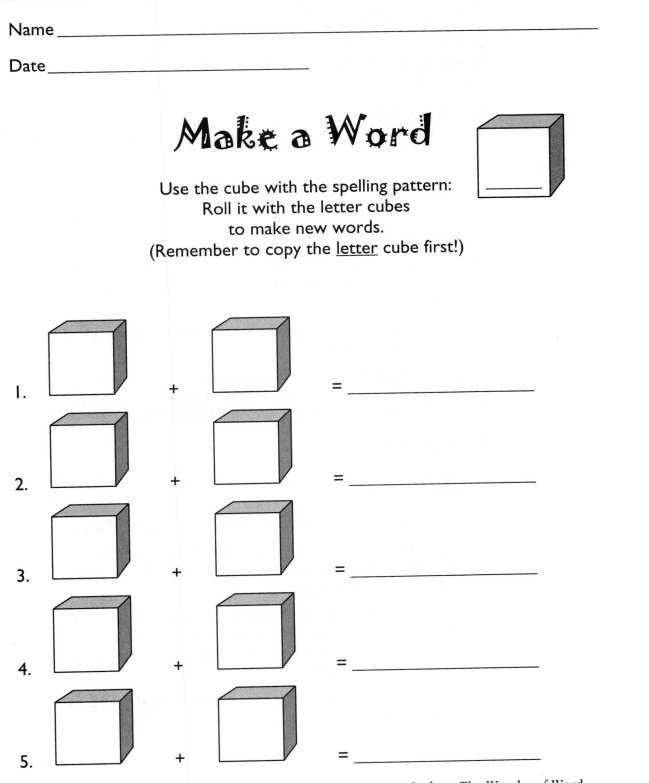

1. ☐ + ☐ = _____

2. ☐ + ☐ = _____

3. ☐ + ☐ = _____

4. ☐ + ☐ = _____

5. ☐ + ☐ = _____

FIGURE 8–3: Make a Word Worksheet

TITLE: Word Train

PURPOSE: To familiarize children with the commonalities in words and to help them use common spelling patterns to form new words.

MATERIALS NEEDED:

- Word Train worksheet (Figure 8–5)
- pencils
- access to previous spelling pattern work
- folder

PREPARATION AND STORAGE:

1. Make several photocopies of the game worksheet and keep them in a folder with one copy on the cover so children know what's inside.

2. Write a base word that you want your students to begin with in "train car #1."

3. Have a designated area where many words with common spelling patterns are displayed. The children may need to use this as a resource when playing their game.

INSTRUCTIONS:

1. Pair up two children to work together as partners and give them a worksheet.

2. The students should both work on the same piece of paper.

3. After reading the word in "train car #1," they should take turns changing either the first letter or the last letter of the word to form a new word.

4. As each player takes a turn, his or her partner should confirm that the new word written is actually a true word, and then begin to attempt to change the first or last letter of the previous word to spell a new word.

5. When the students have recorded four new words and have finished "train car #5," the game is over.

FIGURE 8–4: Word Train

Word Train

1. Start with the word in train car #1.
2. Change either the first letter or the last letter of the word to create a new word.
3. Write the new word in train car #2.
4. Look at the new word in train car #2 and change either the first or the last letter of the word.
5. Write the new word in train car #3.
6. Keep on going until you have finished each train car.

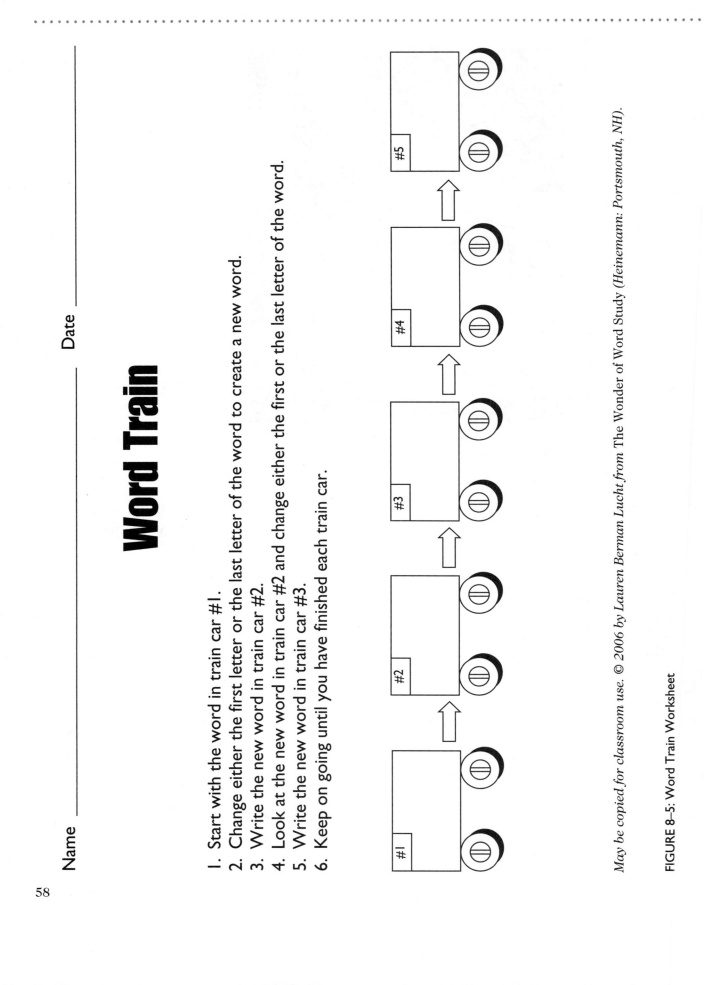

May be copied for classroom use. © 2006 by Lauren Berman Lucht from The Wonder of Word Study (Heinemann: Portsmouth, NH).

FIGURE 8–5: Word Train Worksheet

TITLE: Smile Words

PURPOSE: To remind children of the base words (high-frequency words) that have common spelling patterns and will help them to spell (and read) many other words.

MATERIALS NEEDED:

- Smile Words worksheet (Figure 8–7)
- pencils
- access to previous spelling pattern work
- folder

PREPARATION AND STORAGE:

1. Make several photocopies of the game worksheet and keep them in a folder with one copy on the cover so children know what's inside.

2. Have a designated area where your base words are displayed. This will be where the students can find the "smile words." For example: If you are studying the high-frequency word *went*, either write the word *went* on a card and put it in a plastic baggie with other high-frequency words or write the word *went* on a card and put it on your word wall.

3. Place a smiley face sticker (you can also use a star and change the name of the game to Star Words) on the cards that have base words on them (for example: *went*). These stickers will remind children that the high-frequency words will help them to spell other words.

INSTRUCTIONS:

1. Pair up two children to work together as partners and give them one worksheet to share.

2. The students should choose one base word, from either the word wall or baggie of words that has a smile sticker on it.

3. After recording the word they chose on the space provided at the top of their worksheet, they should take turns changing one letter of the previous word to form a new word.

4. As each player takes a turn, they should only change one letter of the word their partner spelled the turn before theirs. (For example: the pair can start at *went*, change it to *sent*, change it to *send,* and then change it to *sand*.)

5. When the students have recorded as many new words as they can think of, the game is over.

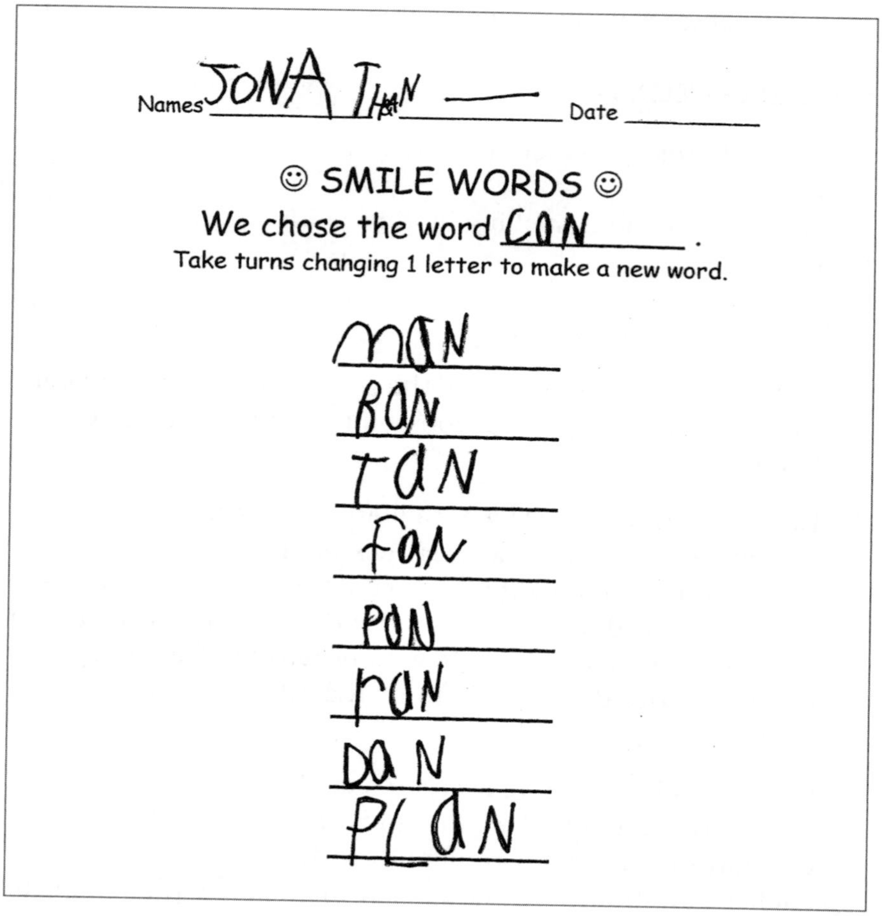

Names JONA THAN ——— Date _____

☺ SMILE WORDS ☺
We chose the word C O N .
Take turns changing 1 letter to make a new word.

MAN
BAN
TAN
FAN
PAN
RAN
DAN
PLAN

FIGURE 8–6: Smile Words

Names _____ & _____

Date_____

☺ Smile Words ☺

We chose the word _____ .
Take turns changing one letter to make a new word.

_____ .

_____

_____

_____

_____

_____

_____

FIGURE 8–7: Smile Words Worksheet

TITLE: Word Wall Word Find

PURPOSE: To practice with sight words, helping children write and recognize learned sight words (or word wall words).

MATERIALS NEEDED:

- Word Wall Word Find worksheet (Figure 8–9)
- pencils
- access to the word wall
- folder

PREPARATION AND STORAGE:

1. Make several photocopies of the game worksheet and keep them in a folder with one copy on the cover so children know what's inside.
2. Make sure that the students have access to the word wall— they should either be able to see the words clearly from their seats or be able to walk up to it and copy their words down.

INSTRUCTIONS:

1. Pair up two children to work together as partners and give each a worksheet.

2. The students choose six words from the word wall and write them on the lines at the bottom of the worksheet.

3. The students then write the words in the boxes—either horizontally, vertically, or diagonally.

4. After filling in the words to find, the students hide the words by placing random letters in all the remaining boxes. (They should make sure to stick to either uppercase or lowercase letters throughout the puzzle.)

5. When they are ready, the students switch papers with their partners and try to find the hidden words. They should keep track of the words they find by crossing them off on the bottom as they go.

6. When they are done, the students can switch their papers back and correct each other's work.

FIGURE 8–8: "Word Wall" Word Find

"Word Wall" Word Find

Directions: Go to the word wall and choose six words to hide. Write the words in the boxes below either across, down, or diagonally. Fill the rest of the boxes in with other letters. Switch papers with a partner to try and find all the hidden words.

<table>
<tr><td></td><td></td><td></td><td></td><td></td><td></td><td></td><td></td></tr>
<tr><td></td><td></td><td></td><td></td><td></td><td></td><td></td><td></td></tr>
<tr><td></td><td></td><td></td><td></td><td></td><td></td><td></td><td></td></tr>
<tr><td></td><td></td><td></td><td></td><td></td><td></td><td></td><td></td></tr>
<tr><td></td><td></td><td></td><td></td><td></td><td></td><td></td><td></td></tr>
<tr><td></td><td></td><td></td><td></td><td></td><td></td><td></td><td></td></tr>
<tr><td></td><td></td><td></td><td></td><td></td><td></td><td></td><td></td></tr>
<tr><td></td><td></td><td></td><td></td><td></td><td></td><td></td><td></td></tr>
</table>

WORDS TO FIND:

_____   _____   _____

_____   _____   _____

FIGURE 8–9: "Word Wall" Word Find Worksheet

TITLE: Word Wall Bingo

PURPOSE: To practice with sight words, helping children to read, write, and recognize learned sight words (or word wall words).

MATERIALS NEEDED:

- Word Wall Bingo worksheet (Figure 8–10)
- pencils
- access to the word wall
- folder
- large pointer

PREPARATION AND STORAGE:

1. Make several photocopies of the game worksheet and keep them in a folder with one copy on the cover so children know what's inside.
2. Make sure that the students have access to the word wall. They should either be able to see the words clearly from their seats, or be able to walk up to it and copy their words down.

INSTRUCTIONS:

1. Pair up three to four children to work together as a group and instruct each to get a worksheet.
2. The students should decide who is going to be the "leader" or the "teacher" first.
3. The remaining two or three students should choose nine words from the word wall and write them in the boxes on their worksheet.
4. When everyone is ready, the leader points to a word on the word wall and reads it aloud. The other students must look on their sheet to see if they have that word written down.
5. If a child has the word that was called out, she crosses it off with a pencil. If the child does not have the word, he sits and waits for the next word to be called.
6. The leader again points to a word and reads it aloud. The game is continued until one player has all nine words on his sheet crossed off.
7. If a player has all her words crossed off, she should yell out "Bingo." The other children must stop while the winner reads off all the words on her sheet and the game is over. If the winner is unable to read all of his nine words, the game may continue with the other players attempting to finish their sheet. (The original winner may choose to watch the game finish or get a new sheet and start again.)

Word Wall Bingo

Choose nine words from the Word Wall
and write them in the boxes below.

FIGURE 8–10: Word Wall Bingo Worksheet

TITLE: Making Words (Adapted from *Making Words* by Patricia Cunningham [1994])

PURPOSE: To help children think about how words work—what letters go together to spell words.

MATERIALS NEEDED:

- Making Words worksheet (Figure 8–12)
- scissors
- pencil
- folder

PREPARATION AND STORAGE:

1. Make several photocopies of the game worksheet and keep them in a folder with one copy on the cover so children know what's inside.

2. Think of a six-letter word for the children to work with. Scramble the letters and write them inside the boxes. (You can prepare a sheet with seven boxes for a greater challenge.)

3. You may want to have your own list of good six-letter words to use with all the combinations of words that can be spelled from it.

INSTRUCTIONS:

1. Pair up two children to work together as partners.

2. The students will begin cutting up the letters of their six-letter word and placing them on the table in front of them.

3. The students will look for small words among the six letters, putting letters together that often help to spell words. (For example: putting st- together could be a possible start but putting ns together will not be helpful in trying to spell words.)

4. As the students find words within the six-letter word, they will begin to record their words on the lines on the worksheet.

5. When the students find as many words as they can, they will try and spell the original six-letter word.

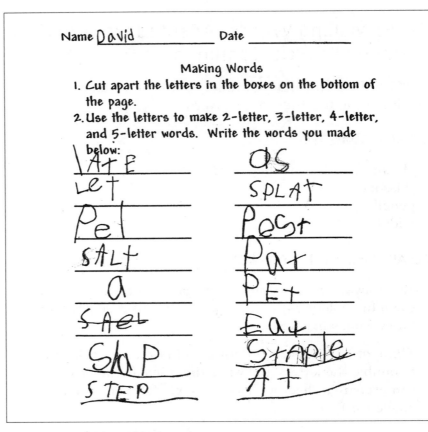

FIGURE 8–11: Making Words

Names _____ & _____

Date _____

Making Words

1. Cut apart the letters in the boxes on the bottom of the page.
2. Use the letters to make two-letter, three-letter, four-letter, and five-letter words. Write the words you made below:

_____   _____

_____   _____

_____   _____

_____   _____

_____   _____

_____   _____

_____   _____

Don't forget to look for common letter combinations as you move the boxes around to create new words.

FIGURE 8–12: Making Words Worksheet

TITLE: Stamp It Out

Purpose: To help children look at specific spelling patterns and use letter stamps to practice spelling the words.

MATERIALS NEEDED:

- Stamp It Out worksheet (Figures 8–13, 8–14)
- letter stamps—upper and lowercase
- stamp pad
- folder

PREPARATION AND STORAGE:

1. You can either make up many different versions of the worksheet (with various spelling patterns) and keep them all in one folder, or you can create and hand out the worksheets on a daily basis. If you choose to keep them all in one folder, make sure to label the folder or glue one copy on the cover so children know what's inside.

2. Store all the letter stamps and ink pads together in a plastic tub and label it "Stamp It Out."

INSTRUCTIONS:

1. Pair up two children to work together as partners.

2. The students should be assigned to work on a specific spelling pattern and should either go and find the appropriate worksheet or request it from the teacher (if they are not all stored together in one folder).

3. The students should either take turns or each work on their own sheet, spelling the words listed in the column.

4. As the students find their stamps and begin recording the words on their worksheet, they will begin to notice that they are using some of the same letters over and over again (the spelling pattern). They should recognize the letters in the spelling pattern that stay the same to help them spell their entire list of words.

5. After stamping out each word on the list, the students should read back all the words they spelled.

Name ______________________________ Date ______________

Stamp It Out

Use the letter stamps to stamp out the following -at words.

bat	___ ___ ___
cat	___ ___ ___
rat	___ ___ ___
sat	___ ___ ___
hat	___ ___ ___
fat	___ ___ ___
Pat	___ ___ ___
mat	___ ___ ___
that	___ ___ ___ ___
chat	___ ___ ___ ___

This chart is just one example of a Stamp It Out worksheet. You can make your own using different spelling patterns by creating a table with two columns and listing the words you would like your students to spell.

FIGURE 8–13: Stamp It Out Worksheet

Name ______________________ Date ____________

Stamp It Out

Use the letter stamps to stamp out the following -ea words.

sea	___ ___ ___
read	___ ___ ___ ___
bean	___ ___ ___ ___
ear	___ ___ ___
hear	___ ___ ___ ___
flea	___ ___ ___ ___
eat	___ ___ ___
ream	___ ___ ___ ___
feast	___ ___ ___ ___ ___
easel	___ ___ ___ ___ ___

Level 2

This chart is just one example of a Stamp It Out worksheet. You can make your own using different spelling patterns by creating a table with two columns and listing the words you would like your students to spell.

FIGURE 8–14: Stamp It Out Worksheet

TITLE: Word Detective

PURPOSE: To help children focus on words surrounding their learning environment while practicing their alphabet letter and sound recognition.

MATERIALS NEEDED:

- Word Detective worksheet (Figure 8–16)
- pencils
- clipboards
- folder

PREPARATION AND STORAGE:

1. Make several photocopies of the game worksheet and keep them in a folder with one copy on the cover so children know what's inside.
2. Choose a letter for the children to go around the room and "detect" and write it in the space provided on the worksheet.

INSTRUCTIONS:

1. Each child (best if played by two or three students) playing may search for words with the same letter or they can be assigned all different letters.

2. The students should look for their assigned letter in words all around the classroom. They can use charts, labels, book titles, name tags, etc., but they should be somewhat aware of what the words say.

3. While searching the room for their assigned letter, they should record its position within the word. They should write the word that contains their letter in the appropriate column on their worksheet. For example: If they are looking for the letter *r* and find it in the word *read*, they should write the word *read* in the first column because the letter *r* is at the beginning of the word. If they also find the letter *r* in the word *chair*, they should write the word *chair* in the last column because the letter *r* comes at the end of the word.

4. The game is over when the students cannot find any more words that contain their assigned letter.

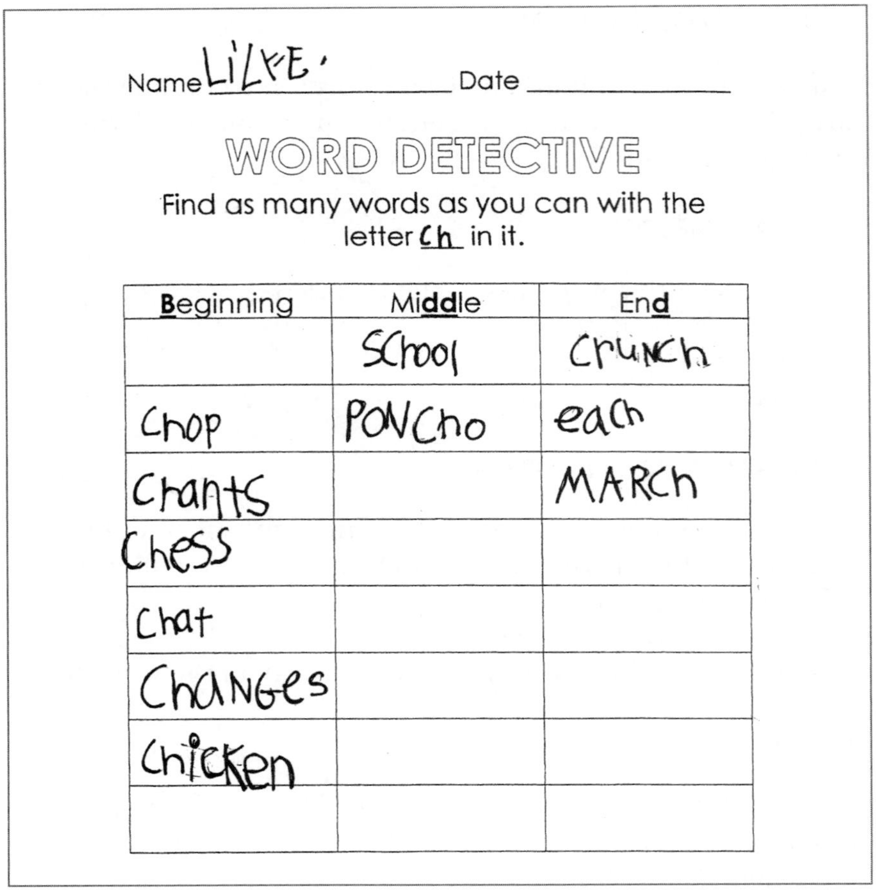

Name LiLvE.   Date _____

WORD DETECTIVE

Find as many words as you can with the
letter **ch** in it.

Beginning	Middle	End
	School	Crunch
Chop	PONCho	each
Chants		MARCh
Chess		
Chat		
Changes		
Chicken		

FIGURE 8–15: Word Detective

Word Detective

Find as many words as you can
with the letter (or letters) _____ in it.

Beginning	Mi**dd**le	En**d**
_____	_____	_____
_____	_____	_____
_____	_____	_____
_____	_____	_____
_____	_____	_____

FIGURE 8–16: Word Detective Worksheet

TITLE: Sound Hunt

PURPOSE: To help children look for and begin to use different variations of spelling for one sound. Also to begin to think of rules that may apply to the correct spelling of those words.

MATERIALS NEEDED:

- Sound Hunt worksheets (Figures 8–17, 8–18)
- pencils
- access to books, magazines, and newspapers
- folder
- clipboards

PREPARATION AND STORAGE:

1. Make several photocopies of the game worksheet and keep them in a folder with one copy on the cover so children know what's inside.

2. Decide which sound hunt you want your students to work on and write it on the sheet in the space provided.

3. Make sure there are plenty of appropriate books, magazines, or newspapers accessible for the children to use to hunt for words.

INSTRUCTIONS:

1. This can be a whole-class or small-group activity. Either way, pair up two children to work together as partners.

2. The students should both work on the same piece of paper.

3. After searching for words, the players record their discoveries on the sheet, making sure to write the original word they found in the column that matches its spelling.

4. When they have found at least ten words they can begin to look for commonalities among the words and try to come up with specific rules the words may follow.

5. The groups can share their findings with the class and continue to work the next day to confirm, adjust, or refute their spelling rules.

Names _____ & _____

Date _____

Sound Hunt

Find words that you hear the e sound in. You can look in books, magazines, newspapers, or around the classroom. Write them in the columns that match the spelling below.

ee	ea	e	y

Did you find any commonalities? Can you make any rules?

_____

_____

_____

_____

FIGURE 8–17: Sound Hunt Worksheet

Names _____ & _____

Date_____

Sound Hunt

Find words that you hear the _____ sound in. You can look in books, magazines, newspapers, or around the classroom. Write them in the columns that match the spelling below.

_____	_____	_____	_____

Did you find any commonalities? Can you make any rules?

_____

_____

_____

_____

FIGURE 8–18: Sound Hunt Worksheet

TITLE: Make Your Own Word Find

PURPOSE: To practice with spelling patterns, helping children to write and recognize learned spelling patterns.

MATERIALS NEEDED:

- Make Your Own Word Find worksheet (Figure 8–19)
- pencils
- access to previous spelling pattern work
- folder

PREPARATION AND STORAGE:

1. Make several photocopies of the game worksheet and keep them in a folder with one copy on the cover so children know what's inside.

2. Choose a spelling pattern for the students to work on and write it in the space provided on the student worksheets.

3. Make sure that the students have access to any spelling pattern work that has been done in class. They may need this as a reference. (You can prepare index cards with lists of words that have the same spelling pattern and keep them in the folder with the worksheets.)

INSTRUCTIONS:

1. Pair up two children to work together as partners and instruct them to get their own worksheet.

2. The students look at the spelling pattern that was chosen for them, think of four words that have the selected spelling pattern, and write them on the lines at the bottom of the worksheet.

3. The students then write the words in the boxes, either horizontally, vertically, or diagonally.

4. After filling in the words to find, the students hide the words by placing random letters in all the remaining boxes. (They should make sure to stick to either uppercase or lowercase letters throughout the puzzle.)

5. When they are ready, the students switch papers with their partner and try to find the hidden words. They should keep track of the words they find by crossing them off on the bottom as they go.

6. When they are done, the students can switch their papers back and correct each other's work.

Make Your Own Word Find

Use the spelling pattern: _____

Directions: Think of four words with the above spelling pattern. Write the words to find on the lines below. Then, spell the words in the boxes below either across, down, or diagonally. Fill the rest of the boxes in with other letters. Switch papers with a partner and try to find all the hidden words!

WORDS TO FIND:

_____   _____

_____   _____

FIGURE 8–19: Make Your Own Word Find Worksheet

TITLE: Word Hunt

PURPOSE: To help children recognize the different sounds a particular spelling pattern can make when found in different words.

MATERIALS NEEDED:

- Word Hunt worksheet (Figure 8–20)
- pencils
- clipboards
- folder
- access to books, magazines, and posters (or any other familiar resource where they can find words)

PREPARATION AND STORAGE:

1. Make several photocopies of the game worksheet and keep them in a folder with one copy on the cover so children know what's inside.

2. Choose a spelling pattern that has more than one common sound and ask the children to "hunt" for it around the room. Write that spelling pattern (as well as both its sounds) in the spaces provided on the worksheet.

3. Prepare a basket of children's magazines, newspapers, or posters with words written in large print.

INSTRUCTIONS:

1. Each child (best if played by two or three students) playing may search for words but they should record their words on only one worksheet.

2. The students can look for their assigned spelling pattern in words all around the classroom. They can use charts, labels, book titles, name tags, etc.

3. As students find their first few words with the correct spelling pattern they listen for the sound the spelling pattern makes and record the word under the appropriate column on their worksheet. (Because of the nature of the game, the students will need to be able to read the words they find.)

4. The game is over when the students cannot find any more words that contain their assigned spelling pattern.

5. As a challenge, ask the students if they notice anything about the words in each column. (Any similarities?)

Word Hunt

Go on a hunt for words that have _____ in them. Look in books, on posters, and around the room. Do your best to read the word and put it in the right box.

Sounds like _____	Sounds like _____

FIGURE 8–20: Word Hunt Worksheet

TITLE: Word Ending Detective
(Adapted from *Spelling K–8* by Diane Snowball and Faye Bolton [1999].)

PURPOSE: To help children recognize interesting endings of words and begin to think of rules that may apply to the spelling of those words.

MATERIALS NEEDED:

- Word Ending Detective worksheet (Figures 8–21, 8–22)
- pencils
- access to books, magazines, and newspapers
- folder
- clipboards

PREPARATION AND STORAGE:

1. Make several photocopies of the game worksheet and keep them in a folder with one copy on the cover so children know what's inside.

2. Decide if you want your students to work on a general word ending detective sheet or a specific one (if you want them to work on a specific word ending, write the ending on the sheet in the space provided).

3. Make sure there are plenty of appropriate books, magazines, or newspapers accessible for the children to use to hunt for words.

INSTRUCTIONS:

1. This can be a whole-class or small-group activity. Either way, pair up two children to work together as partners and instruct them to get a worksheet.

2. The students both work on the same worksheet.

3. After searching for words, the players record their discoveries on the sheet, making sure to write the original word they found, the base word, and the ending.

4. When they have found at least six words they can begin to look for commonalities among the words and try to come to conclusions about specific rules the words may follow.

5. The groups can share their findings with the class and continue to work the next day to confirm, adjust, or refute their spelling rules.

Name ______________________________ Date ______________

Word Ending Detective

Search for words that have interesting endings in books, newspapers, or around the room. List them in the chart below.

WORD	BASE WORD	ENDING
Ex: running	run	ing
Ex: grabbed	grab	ed

Categorize any words that have commonalities below:

______________________ ______________________

______________________ ______________________

______________________ ______________________

______________________ ______________________

______________________ ______________________

FIGURE 8–21: Word Ending Detective Worksheet

Name ______________________________ Date ______________

Word Ending Detective

Search for words, that have an ___ ending, in books, newspapers, or around the room. List them in the chart below.

WORD	BASE WORD	ENDING
Ex:		

Categorize any words that have commonalities below:

________________________ ________________________

________________________ ________________________

Were you able to come up with any specific rules about adding ___ to the end of a word?

____

____

FIGURE 8–22: Word Ending Detective Worksheet

TITLE: Spelling Pattern Detective

PURPOSE: To help children focus on specific spelling patterns surrounding their learning environment while practicing their spelling of familiar words. (This game can be modified to fit any word study inquiry. You can change the game to "Contraction Detective" and continue to play as explained below.)

MATERIALS NEEDED:

- Spelling Pattern Detective worksheet (Figure 8–23)
- pencils
- clipboards
- folder

PREPARATION AND STORAGE:

1. Make several photocopies of the game worksheet and keep them in a folder with one copy on the cover so children know what's inside.
2. Choose a spelling pattern for the children to "detect" around the room and write it in the space provided on the worksheet.

INSTRUCTIONS:

1. Each child (best if played by two or three students) playing may search for words with the same spelling pattern, or they can be assigned different ones.

2. The students look for their assigned spelling pattern in words all around the classroom. They can use charts, labels, book titles, name tags, etc., but they should be somewhat aware of what the words say.

3. While searching the room for their assigned spelling pattern, the students record their words on the worksheet.

4. The game is over when the students cannot find any more words that contain their assigned spelling pattern.

Name _____

Date _____

Spelling Pattern Detective

Go on a word hunt and look for words with the _____ spelling pattern.

Here are the words I found . . .

_____

_____

_____

_____

_____

_____

_____

FIGURE 8–23: Spelling Pattern Detective Worksheet

TITLE: The Spelling Pattern Game

PURPOSE: To help children look at various spelling patterns and use different mediums to explore words that can be spelled from them.

MATERIALS NEEDED:

- The Spelling Pattern Game worksheet (Figure 8–24)
- pencils
- access to previous spelling pattern work
- folder
- various manipulatives: playdough, magnetic letters, letter dice, block letters, chalk and chalkboards, wipe-off markers and boards

PREPARATION AND STORAGE:

1. Make several photocopies of the game worksheet and keep them in a folder with one copy on the cover so children know what's inside.

2. Any manipulatives that you would use for this game should be stored in a bag or tub and can be labeled "For the Spelling Pattern Game."

3. Erasers or tissues should be made available if the children are going to use chalk or wipe-off markers.

INSTRUCTIONS:

1. Pair up two children to work together as partners and instruct them to get a worksheet.

2. The students begin their exploration of a spelling pattern by first deciding what spelling pattern to begin with and then either spelling it with manipulatives, creating it with playdough, or writing it with chalk or markers.

3. Once students have the spelling pattern in front of them, they record it in pencil on their worksheet in the space provided.

4. After recording the spelling pattern, they begin to put new letters in front of the spelling pattern to make new words.

5. They can record each new word on their worksheet until they cannot think of any more.

6. When they are through with the first spelling-pattern exploration, the students decide on one more and choose a new manipulative to practice spelling it with.

7. The students continue to play the game until the bottom portion is filled out and they cannot think of any more words that have the same spelling pattern.

Name _____

Date _____

The Spelling Pattern Game

I used the spelling pattern _____ to make these new words:

_____   _____   _____

_____   _____   _____

_____   _____   _____

I also used the spelling pattern _____ to make these new words:

_____   _____   _____

_____   _____   _____

_____   _____   _____

FIGURE 8–24: The Spelling Pattern Game Worksheet

A Walk Through a Word Study Lesson

I invite you to join my class as we are about to begin our word study lesson for the day. As you enter the room, you will notice that the children are sitting on a large rug in front of an easel. I am sitting in a chair facing the children and holding a big book on the easel. The children are silent, waiting to hear what the day's lesson will entail. They are familiar with the structure of our lessons and are prepared to participate. As you read the next few pages, I ask you to try and imagine that you are sitting in the back of the room watching the class. Part of the lesson will be spelled out for you directly. Other parts, you will need to read my explanations to understand what has just happened. Please be sure to read the other sample lessons throughout the book for more detailed student/teacher interaction.

Focus of the Lesson

Recognizing the sight word *not* and using it to read and spell other words.

Introduction

"Yesterday we read the book *Who Will Help?* by Rozanne Williams and Mary Thelen and we practiced *framing* the word *not*. Let's read a couple of pages to remember."

Teacher note—The children are called up to frame the word *not*. The third time someone comes up to the easel, the word *not* is in a new placement on the page. If the opportunity exists, it's a good idea to challenge the students to recognize the word in a different spot in the book, focusing them on the actual letters in the word and not the placement of it within a text.

Minilesson

(Five minutes including the introduction)

"Today we're going to reread the book *Cooking Pot* by Joy Cowley and this time, really listen for the words that sound like *not*."

Teacher note—It's a good idea to have read the book previous to beginning the word study lesson. This way, the *reading* of the book is not the challenge or the focus of the minilesson. In the meantime, a good teacher always slips some new teaching points into everything she does. I take the opportunity to compliment Mason as he reads with correct fluency, encouraging the other students to remember that exclamation marks don't necessarily mean they should read loudly but rather with excitement or interest. Also, the last page of the book contains large, bold text. As the children read it with extra enthusiasm, I compliment their attention to the special text feature.

Making the Connection

"Yesterday Elie told us that *not* had a *spelling pattern* in it. What is the spelling pattern?"

Teacher note—I like to repeat my purpose more than once in a lesson. Even though the children already understand that -ot is the spelling pattern, I remind them that -ot is the part of the word that stays the same and helps us to spell other words. This language will help them transfer their learning to their independent work.

Student Interaction

(Eight minutes including the connection)

The students offer other words that sound like *not* and come up to spell them with magnetic letters on the easel.

Teacher note—If a child is struggling to think of a word, it's good to remind him to go back to the book he just read and think of one from there. During the lesson, this happens with Joe. As soon as I mention the book he thinks of the word *pot*. Also, it's a good idea to only put up magnetic letters that the children are going to be successful with. If a child is trying to think of a word, she can look at the line of letters on the easel and begin to replace the letter *n* in *not* with another letter that is up there.

Workshop Activities

(10 minutes)

As the children are asked to leave the rug and continue the learning on their own (through games and activities), I ask that you try and imagine you are still in my classroom observing the students. The children are dismissed from the rug, one by one, while being assigned to their workshop activities.

As I mentioned in Chapter 3, there are three important components to a successful workshop:

- organization
- tone
- independence

Look for evidence of this while observing the class. Notice that the room is organized so the children are able to get started on their games immediately without the help of an adult. There is one particular section of the room dedicated to word games. The children are aware of where their games are located and can easily sort through the correct baskets or shelves to find what's needed. Also, the room is alive with chatter about their games but quiet enough that everyone is able to speak in a comfortable tone. Because my routines have already been set, the children are aware that if I am sitting at the circle table with a student, we are not to be disturbed. Only when I am walking around the room checking in on the other students are they free to speak with me.

While the other students are working, I choose two children to work with for a guided word study group. These two students are already good spellers but sometimes forget to use what they already know to help them spell new words. They memorize spellings and can usually recognize when something is correct. But when trying to spell a word they've never seen before, they struggle with listening for chunks or spelling patterns that they know. I chose the activity to help them play with letters—making common chunks and spelling patterns—and then seeing what words they can spell from them. I adapted this game from Patricia Cunningham's book *Making Words* to fit the needs of my young students. David and Libby use the original word *forest* to find other words using different letter combinations. (This is much like the games in newspapers or puzzle books where you must see how many words you can spell using the letters in the given word. The difference is, you're not looking to see how *many* words you can spell, but what patterns you can create within the letters to form strategies that help you spell new words.) Examples of many of the children's work from this (or previous) workshop time are included in Chapter 8.

Special Notes About the Lesson

It's important to model different learning strategies that you want your students to use on their own. This happens quite a bit during the lesson.

● Max suggests *a lot* as one word that sounds like *not*. Rather than explain that it is actually two words, I show him the page in the book where it says, "Thanks a lot, Mrs. Spot." He immediately understands that the word is actually just *lot*, and I've suggested a way for him to discover this on his own in the future.

● When Isabella offers the word *blot* as a word to spell, I ask her if she knows what it means. Another student suggests that we look it up in the dictionary—obviously remembering that this is a strategy we use sometimes. It's great to model using a dictionary in front of young children. Also, they learn that even I don't know the meaning of (or how to spell) every word! It helps them to connect with you as their teacher and appreciate that learning never ends.

● When Isabella eventually does approach the easel to spell the word *blot* with magnetic letters, she grabs a lowercase *d* to begin. Then she does the smartest thing—she looks above my head at the alphabet chart hanging on the wall. She is holding the letter up to compare it with the lowercase *b* above. As she realizes that she has the wrong letter, I comment to the class, explaining what she's done. Catching those smart moments and pointing them out to all the students makes word study learning exciting and successful.

So many teaching points can come up within one short minilesson. Although the most important thing is that you stick to your focus and repeat your purpose, it's great to *sneak* other learning into your lessons. During this particular lesson, I notice that I did this at least two or three times. (I'm getting so *sneaky*, I don't even catch myself doing it anymore!)

● When Avery comes up to spell *spot* he puts up the letters *s, o,* and *t*. Rather than correct him, I ask the class to say the word with me while I slide my finger under the letters (getting them to stretch the word out together). The class reads *sot*. Avery immediately puts a *p* in the middle to correct himself. Teaching children to slide their finger under a word and stretch it out aloud helps them catch their mistakes. Shelley Harwayne once told me that she uses this great catchphrase: "This word makes me say *sot*. *Make* me say *spot*." I loved the way she put that and I use the phrase often—Make me say _____. It really helps the children understand that the reason to spell correctly is to get people to read exactly what we want them to.

● Jack approaches the easel to spell the word *slot*. He spells it with a capital *S*. When I ask him why, he says that a capital is for a name (we've been learning this). I ask him if the word *slot* is a name. As soon as he says, "no," he switches the letter to a lowercase *s*. This was a quick review of when to use a capital letter at the beginning of a word.

● Erica wants to spell *shot*. Because sh- can be difficult for young children, I find every opportunity to accentuate the sh- sound. I put my finger to my lips and make a sound as if I am asking the children to be quiet. The more ways you can physically represent sounds, the better the children will remember them. (For example: stick your tongue out for the sound th- makes, pucker your lips to make the sound of wh-, etc.)

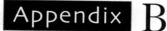

Blending and Segmenting Assessments

I am going to say a word slowly and I want you to try and guess what word I'm saying. Let's practice: *c-a-t*. Can you guess that word? That's right, it's *cat*. Now let's try more.

1. th-i-ck
2. r-a-ke
3. s-a-n-d
4. tr-u-ck
5. p-l-a-te
6. s-tr-ee-t
7. m-ou-se

Now I am going to say a word and I want you to try and say it slowly and break it up into different sounds. Let's try one together. Let's break up the word *game*: g-a-me. Now you try the rest.

1. pen (p-e-n)
2. book (b-oo-k)
3. shop (sh-o-p)
4. cup (c-u-p)
5. house (h-ou-se)
6. clock (c-l-o-ck)
7. dance (d-a-n-ce)

Rhyming Assessment

*R*hyming words are words that sound the same at the end. Listen to how these words rhyme: *fan/van*. Do you hear how they sound the same at the end? Let's try some together: *rug/bug*. Do those words rhyme? Yes, they do. How about *rug/mat*? No, they don't—good. Now let's try more.

1. fan/ran
2. fan/fish
3. rug/mug
4. wall/hall
5. wall/cup
6. ship/clip
7. ship/show
8. night/light
9. small/tall
10. near/knee
11. flower/shower
12. rest/chest

Word Study
Assessment* Checklist

Child's Name _____ Date _____

❏ Recognizes names of all upper- and lowercase letters.

Uppercase letters missed _____.

Lowercase letters missed _____.

❏ Recognizes sounds of all consonant letters and long vowel sounds.

Letter sounds missed _____.

❏ Recognizes short vowel sounds.

❏ Represents all sounds in a word.

❏ Uses learned knowledge of blends and digraphs in the beginning of words.

❏ Uses learned knowledge of blends and digraphs in the middle of words and at the end of words.

❏ Recognizes common spelling patterns in all parts of a word.

❏ Recognizes learned word endings.

❏ Chooses the correct spelling when writing homophones.

❏ Shows signs of a beginning understanding of the use of an apostrophe.

❏ Correctly uses apostrophes for both contractions and possessives.

❏ Beginning mastering of correct spelling of words with added endings (for example: doubles the final consonant, drops the final -e, changes -y to -ies).

❏ Correctly spells learned high-frequency words.

Notes:

_____

_____

*With the exception of the alphabet assessment, I suggest looking at samples of children's writing when using this checklist to inform your teaching.

Appendix E

Blank Workshop Chart

*U*se this chart to help send children off to play their activities quickly and smoothly. Children can refer to the chart to see what game they are to play. The chart will also help you to keep track of what inquiries the children were practicing for the week and where they should go next.

Word Study Workshop

Child's name	Date	Date	Date	Date	Date

Inquiry of the week:

Goals:

Observations:

Homework
Ideas

Many of the games in Chapter 8 can be revised and sent home for additional practice. The homework is fun for children, and their parents get the opportunity to understand your word study program a bit better. In this section I've included a few more examples of games and activities that the students can play at home as a follow-up to your word study inquiries.

Name _____

Date _____

HOMEWORK: Can you think of six words that sound like _____?
Write the words below. Then draw a picture to match your words.

WORDS	PICTURES

Name: MASON   Date: _____

Homework: Can you think of six words that sound like __will__?
Write the words below. Then draw a picture to match your words!

FIGURE A–1: A Student's Practice of –ill Words

Word Find Homework

Name _____

Date _____

Search the puzzle below for words with _____. You will find them horizontally, vertically, and diagonally.

WORDS TO FIND:

_____   _____   _____

_____   _____   _____

_____   _____   _____

Homework Hunt

Name _____

Date _____

While reading for homework tonight, write down any words that struck you. (Maybe the spelling of a word surprised you? Or maybe you've seen the word spelled differently before?)

I was reading _____.

Word	Page #

Titles for Word Study Inquiries

*T*his chart is a suggested list of titles to help you get started with your word study program. I have included many of the poems as examples. Poems that are not included in this book can mostly be found through the Internet. You can go to your favorite search engine and type in the name of the poem and the author. Also, many of the poems (especially those by Linda B. Ross and Helen H. Moore) can be found in various children's poetry anthologies. This chart is a work in progress and should be added to as you discover new titles.

Word Study Inquiries

INQUIRY	BIG BOOK TITLES	POEM TITLES
-an	*Shark in a Sack* by Joy Cowley *Dan the Flying Man* by Joy Cowley *I Can Read/I Can Write* by Rozanne Lanczak Williams *Our Pumpkin* by Renee Keeler	"The Gingerbread House" by Lauren Berman "Happy Clan" by Linda B. Ross
-op	*Stop!* by Joy Cowley	"Apples" by Helen H. Moore "My Shop" by Linda B. Ross
-in	*Making Patterns* by Elizabeth Savage *Ice Cream* by Joy Cowley *Up in a Tree* by Joy Cowley	"Dinnertime" by Lauren Berman
-ay	*We Can Make Graphs* by Rozanne Lanczak Williams *Cookie's Week* by Cindy Ward and Illustrated by Tomie dePaola	"Rain," author unknown "Rainy Day" by William Wise
-at	*The Zoo* by Christine Young *Ratty Tatty* by Joy Cowley *Hats* by Debra Lee	"The Lost Cat" by Shel Silverstein "Caterpillar, Caterpillar" by Susan Seitner

INQUIRY	BIG BOOK TITLES	POEM TITLES
-ice	*Ice Cream* by Joy Cowley *Chicken Soup with Rice* by Maurice Sendak	"January" by Maurice Sendak (from *Chicken Soup with Rice*) "Freckles" by Aileen Fisher
-ike	*Ice Cream* by Joy Cowley *A Day at School* by Jillian Cutting *Microscope* by Joy Cowley *What Would You Like?* by Joy Cowley	"Waiting for Fall" by Lauren Berman
-ump	*Mr. Grump* by Joy Cowley *I Can Jump* by Joy Cowley	"Frogs and Toads" by Lauren Berman
-own	*Down to Town* by Joy Cowley *To Town* by Joy Cowley	"The Happy Princess" by Lauren Berman
-ow	*The Pink Balloon* by Clare Bowes	"Winter Wind" by Lauren Berman "Dandelions" by Marietta W. Brewster
-ad	*When Lana Was Absent* by Robert Avitabile	"Never Mind March," author unknown
-ent	*Mrs. Wishy-Washy* by Joy Cowley *Stop!* by Joy Cowley *The Red Rose* by Joy Cowley	"Shopping" by Lauren Berman
-ap	*Ratty Tatty* by Joy Cowley	"Sampan" by Tao Lang Pee
-ot	*The Cooking Pot* by Joy Cowley *What Is a Huggles?* by Joy Cowley *Forgetful Fred* by Andrea Butler *Who Will Help?* Adapted by Rozanne Lanczak Williams	"Pease Porridge" (Mother Goose rhyme) "Tea Party" by Helen O'Reilly "Mail" by Lauren Berman
-ick	*Amazing Magnets* by Gloria Bancroft *Tricking Tracy* by Sue Donovan and Andrea Butler	"Ick, Ick, Ick" by Kelley Lucht
-ouse	*Our Street* by Joy Cowley	"The Chase" by Angelin Lucht
-og	*Frog on a Log* by Norma L. Gentner	"Frog" by Lauren Berman
-eet	*Feet* by Henry Layne and Kathy Hoggan	"Spring Is Here" by Lauren Berman
-ake	*The Birthday Cake* by Joy Cowley *Along Comes Jake* by Joy Cowley	"Birthday Cake" by Lauren Berman
-ug	*A Hug Is Warm* by Joy Cowley	"What I Saw" by Helen O'Reilly "Mr. Ladybug" by Helen H. Moore
-and	*Hands, Hands, Hands* by Marcia Vaughan *Snowman* by Joy Cowley	"Sand Castle" by Lauren Berman
-ill	*To Town* by Joy Cowley	"Wintertime" by Meish Goldish "November" by Lauren Berman "Jack and Jill" (Mother Goose rhyme) "At My Windowsill" by Linda B. Ross
-ate	*The Hungry Giant's Lunch* by Joe Cowley *Excuses, Excuses* by Andrea Butler	"A Date to Skate" by Linda B. Ross
-ight	*It Didn't Frighten Me* by Janet L. Gross and Jerome C. Harste	"My Aquarium" by Christopher Lucht
-all		"Humpty Dumpty" (Mother Goose rhyme) "Fall is Here" by Helen H. Moore
-id	*Wishy Washy Day* by Joy Cowley	"The Auction" by Kelley Lucht
-it	*My Shadow* by Jillian Cutting	"My Dog Kit" by Linda B. Ross
-ook	*The Zoo* by Christine Young	"Books" by Helen H. Moore

continues

INQUIRY	BIG BOOK TITLES	POEM TITLES
-ell		"The Pumpkin Eater" (Mother Goose rhyme) "Where Is Nell?" by Linda B. Ross
th-	*Along Comes Jake* by Joy Cowley	"The Mitten Song" by Marie Louise Allen "In Tune with June" by Helen H. Moore

-ed	*Five Little Monkeys*, chosen by Anne
	    Hanzel and illustrated by Majory Gardner
	The Dandelion by Brian and Jillian Cutting
	The Best Children in the World by
	    Joy Cowley
	Mr. Noisy by Rozanne Lanczak Williams
	The Pumpkin by Joy Cowley
	What's Cooking? by Shelley Harwayne
	Whoosh by Joy Cowley
	Mr. Grump by Joy Cowley
		"Cat and the Fiddle" (Mother Goose rhyme)
		"School Daze Rap" by Carol Diggory Shields

-ing	*The Jigaree* by Joy Cowley	"Spider" by Lilian Moore "Spring" by Karla Kuskin "Go Wind" by Lilian Moore
sh-	*Who Lives in the Sea* by Sylvia M. James	"Fishing Trip" by Lauren Berman
br-	*Splishy-Sploshy* by Joy Cowley	"Dog Park" by Angelin Lucht
gr-	*Mr. Grump* by Joy Cowley	"The Greedy Grasshopper" by Lauren Berman
dr-		"My Dream" by Lauren Berman
tr-	*Tricking Tracy* by Sue Donovan and Andrea Butler	"City Child" by Lois Lensky
sp-	*How Spiders Live* by Fred and Jeanne Biddulph *The Very Busy Spider* by Eric Carle	"Family Rules" by Angelin Lucht "I Spy" by Angelin Lucht
st-	*Stop!* by Joy Cowley *The Magic Stick* by Barbara Shook Hazen	"Safety" by Helen H. Moore
ch-	*Munching Mark* by Elizabeth Cannard and her class	"Birds in the Spring" by Lori McGinnis
gl-		"Ocean's Beauty" by Lauren Berman
-er	*The Scrubbing Machine* by Joy Cowley *Crunchy Munchy* by Brenda Parkes *The Terrible Tiger* by Joy Cowley	"School" by Lauren Berman "Careers" by Paula Peck "Invitation" by Shel Silverstein
-y	*Hairy Bear* by Joy Cowley	"Tea Party" by Helen O'Reilly "I'm Really Neat" author unknown "The Chase" by Angelin Lucht
Compound Words	*Rainbows and Moonbeams* by Jill Carter and Judy Ling	"My Good Old Backpack" by Betsy Franco
Apostrophes		"The Mail Carrier" by Lauren Berman "November" by Lauren Berman

Word Study
Inquiry Poetry

Word Study Inquiry:

gl-

OCEAN'S BEAUTY

Have you ever been as lucky as me
To watch a dolphin glide in the sea?

Their glamorous bodies
    dive way down deep.
Then dance on their tails—
    their balance they keep.

Gray skin glistens in the sunlight.
But what a treat to see one at night.

The moon glows on the silvery ocean,
While the dolphin swims by
    in slow motion.

LAUREN BERMAN

-and

SAND CASTLE

Over by the ocean
In a sea salted land,
Was a tiny little castle
Made only of some sand.

This tiny little castle
With no windows or no door.
Was the grandest of all castles
'Till it washed away from shore.

LAUREN BERMAN

-ent

SHOPPING

My mom sent me out
To buy food from the store
I had plenty of money
I didn't need more.

I went through the aisles
With my list in my hand.
Loaded up the cart,
Paid for my food and . . .

Got 50 cents back.
Wow, I had more money to spend!
I saved it for a day and
Then spent it on a friend.

LAUREN BERMAN

-eet (or -ee)

SPRING IS HERE

Feel the warmth in the air.
See the colors and feet so bare.
Taste the ice cream—cold and sweet.
Hear the birds chirp and tweet.
Spring is here, the day has come,
For all new life and lots of fun.

LAUREN BERMAN

-id

THE AUCTION

Once there was a clever boy
Whose name was "Little Sid."

He had a valuable baseball card
That he wanted to get rid.

At the fancy auction house
He waited for his bid.

The auctioneer was surprised,
His embarrassment he hid.

The highest item of the day
Was sold by a little kid!

KELLEY LUCHT

-ouse

THE CHASE

Little Lady, Little Mouse,
Creeping softly through the house.
Here comes Ratty—Ugly Louse.
Chased her but she got away.
He'll come back another day.

ANGELIN LUCHT

-an

THE GINGERBREAD HOUSE

I made a house that's candy.
It's as sweet as it can be.
My name is the Gingerbread Man,
And this is the house for me!

LAUREN BERMAN

Apostrophes

THE MAIL CARRIER

The mail carrier's bag is full
With letters from 'round the nation.
He then makes sure to bring them
To the nearest postal station.

These letters are delivered
By foot or truck or car.
Sometimes boats and planes help out
In case they're going far!

LAUREN BERMAN

-ike

WAITING FOR FALL

In the fall I like to do
Many different things with you.
In the woods we go for hikes.
On country roads we take our bikes.
Apple picking, collecting leaves,
Can't you bring fall sooner, *please*?

LAUREN BERMAN

-OW

WINTER WIND

Hear that?
See that?
It's the wind—feel it blow?
The winter storm is on it's way.
I think it's bringing snow!
I asked my friend but he's not sure.
Any chance **you** know?

LAUREN BERMAN

-ake

BIRTHDAY CAKE

The best part of a birthday
Is of course the cake.
Any flavor that you choose
The pastry shop will make.
Frosted flowers,
Chocolate filling,
Add more layers
'Till they're spilling,
Out of the pan and ready to bake.
Here it comes . . . **birthday cake!**

LAUREN BERMAN

-in

DINNERTIME

Up in the tree sits
A little black spider,
Waiting to find his dinner.
He spins his web and watches
Waiting,
Baiting,
As other insects come invading.
Into the web they creep and crawl.
Until they can no longer move at all.
The spider wins!
His meal is found.
He eats and then
climbs on back down.

LAUREN BERMAN

br-

DOG PARK

Down by the brook,
Near the red brick wall,
There'll be plenty of space
Bring a bone and a ball.
We'll play Frisbee and fetch.
The fun begins around two.
Take a break and meet us—
The *BOTH* of you.

ANGELIN LUCHT

sp-

FAMILY RULES

Don't splash in puddles
On a rainy spring day.
Don't spoil your supper,
My mom loves to say.
Don't spend all your allowance.
That's Dad's favorite one.
But so many DON'Ts
Takes away all of my fun!

ANGELIN LUCHT

sh-

FISHING TRIP

We sailed away around four
And waved as we left the shore.
I made a wish
To catch a fish
And shouted "Let's get more!"

My dad said it was time to go.
My catch I was excited to show.
But I only got three
How could that be?
I'll wish harder next time, I know.

LAUREN BERMAN

-ump

FROGS AND TOADS

Some toads jump while frogs can leap.
Some have bumps and some can keep
Smooth wet skin
Bright colored or spotted.
Others brown and polka-dotted.
Whether lumpy, smooth or green,
All frogs and toads are amphibians!

LAUREN BERMAN

-og

FROG

Once a tadpole,
Now a frog.
Used to swim
Now sits on logs.

Lives in bogs
Or ponds or rivers.
They may look cute
But make me shiver.

LAUREN BERMAN

gr-

THE GREEDY GRASSHOPPER

The greedy green grasshopper
Had forgotten how to share.
When his friends got mad at him
He answered "I don't care."

One day he forgot to pack a lunch.
His belly began to moan.
Sad and grumpy he grabbed some food.
His friends yelled "Get your own!"

LAUREN BERMAN

-own

THE HAPPY PRINCESS

Ever seen a princess frown?
Or hang her head at all?
For if she would her crown would surely
Slip off her head and fall.
Her jewels would break to pieces
Her favorite bought in town.
So she always holds her head up
And never hangs it down.

LAUREN BERMAN

. . . .

sp-

I SPY

I spy with my very own eye:
A spark in the dark,
And spinach in a can,
A spear in a tree trunk,
And spaghetti in the pan,
A speck in my milk,
And a spoon from my shake,
A sponge in the tub,
And sprinkles on my cake!

ANGELIN LUCHT

-ick

ICK, ICK, ICK

When you come home from school
feeling rather sick;

I know the reason why—
Your fingers you have licked.

You've touched a million things—
much dirtier than a stick.

So, let me tell you kiddies
a secret or a trick . . .

Always wash your hands,
and your noses never pick!

KELLEY LUCHT

-ot

MAIL

Her mailbox is full of letters.
You take a look, but yours is not.
So you write to all your friends
And hope the words will mean a lot.

A stamp will cost you 37 cents.
This might be all you've got.
But when you find your
mailbox stuffed,
Those letters will hit the spot!

LAUREN BERMAN

-ight

MY AQUARIUM

A tank full of fish
Is my favorite sight.
So many bright colors
Swimming under the light.

When feeding time comes
It's just before night.
"There's enough for everyone.
No need to fight!"

LAUREN BERMAN

dr-

MY DREAM

As I closed my eyes last night,
And drifted into dreams,
It slowly started drizzling—
Then raining hard it seemed.

My tent was drenched with water.
The drops slid down the wall.
I had thought that I was dreaming.
But I hadn't been at all.

LAUREN BERMAN

-ill

NOVEMBER

It's November and Fall is here.
Scarecrows and pumpkins and
A chill in the air.

The leaves will change colors
And spill to the ground.
This season's almost over.
Winter's coming around.

LAUREN BERMAN

Books

That I Couldn't Live Without

Cowley, Joy. 1983. *Dan the Flying Man*. New Zealand: Shortland Publications.

Cunningham, Patricia. 1994. *Making Words*. Great Rapids, MI: McGraw-Hill Children's.

Cunningham, Patricia M., and Richard L. Allington. 1994. *Classrooms That Work*. Boston, MA: Allyn & Bacon.

Ericson, Lita, and Moira Fraser Juliebo. 1998. *The Phonological Awareness Handbook for Kindergarten and Primary Teachers*. Newark, DE: International Reading Association.

Fountas, Irene, and Gay Su Pinnel. 1998. *Word Matters: Teaching Phonics and Spelling in the Reading/Writing Classroom*. Portsmouth, NH: Heinemann.

Franzese, Rosalie. 2002. *Reading and Writing in Kindergarten: A Practical Guide*. New York: Scholastic.

Moore, Helen H. 1997. *A Poem a Day: 180 Thematic Poems and Activities That Teach and Delight All Year Long*. New York: Scholastic.

Moustafa, Margaret. 1995. *Whole to Part Phonics: How Children Learn to Read and Spell*. Portsmouth, NH: Heinemann.

———. 1997. *Beyond Traditional Phonics: Research Discoveries and Reading Instruction*. Portsmouth, NH: Heinemann.

Snowball, Diane, and Faye Bolton. 1999. *Spelling K–8: Planning and Teaching*. York, ME: Stenhouse.

Wilen, Jennifer, and Beth Handa. 2002. *70 Wonderful Word Family Poems*. New York: Scholastic.